CYCLING IN THE SIXTIES

CYCLING IN THE SIXTIES

by David Saunders

PELHAM BOOKS

First published in Great Britain
by Pelham Books Ltd
52 Bedford Square
London, W.C.1
1971

7207 0456 1

Set and printed in Great Britain by
Tonbridge Printers Ltd,
Peach Hall Works, Tonbridge, Kent
in Times ten on twelve point, on paper supplied
by P. F. Bingham Ltd, and bound by James Burn
at Esher, Surrey

CONTENTS

Contents

ILLUSTRATIONS

Illustrations

ACKNOWLEDGEMENTS

The author's thanks are due to the following whose photographs are reproduced in this book: *United Press International:* 1, 6; *Len Thorpe:* 2; *Cycling:* 3; *J. R. Otway:* 4, 5, 8, 9, 10, 12, 14; *Central Press Photos:* 7, 16; *Associated Press:* 13; *R. V. Good:* 15.

FOREWORD

By John Bromley

Executive Producer of ITV's 'World of Sport'

I will not forget the day I came face to face with cycling.

At the time, I was writing a column for the *Daily Mirror* and decided that a day's outing on the Tour of Britain (later to become known as the Milk Race) would make interesting copy.

For a new boy to the game, it was a vivid, exciting and, at times, frightening experience. Following the race in one of the many Press cars was like sharing a seat with Graham Hill in a Grand Prix as we screamed around hairpin bends on the wrong side of the road to either keep our place in the cavalcade or leap frog ahead of the leading bunch of riders.

Once ahead of the race, I remember we stopped in a village to calm my shattered nerves with a large scotch and there we stood at the bottom of this steep, cobbled High Street as the world's outstanding amateur road cyclists swept down the hill, moving at 50 miles per hour over the cobbles and showing such skill and courage as they avoided parked cars, aged villagers and stray dogs to maintain their position in that particular stage.

Cycling, I realised on that June day, was a gutsy, competitive sport that had a magic of its own to those who followed it closely.

Since then, my newspaper and television career has seen me sit in the stands at a track meeting; withstand the perils of a Dover to Calais boat crossing to watch the world cyclo-cross championships; scream myself hoarse at a Wembley six-day meeting and travel many a by-way to report the greatest event

9

in the cycling calendar – the Tour de France.

On most of those occasions, my colleague has been David Saunders. As a journalist and television commentator he combines knowledge with enthusiasm. He has become widely recognised as one of the outstanding reporters in cycling because, although he may occasionally criticise rider or official, always his aim is to improve the status of the sport and he, along with many others, cherishes the day when cycling in Britain will have the coverage and spectator appeal that it does on the Continent.

In this book, David Saunders tells of the outstanding moments in world and domestic cycling over the last ten years and he is at his best when writing about the personalities in the game – men like the late Tom Simpson, who was his close personal friend, and of Eddy Merckx, the Pele of cycling.

He gets to the heart of these people and thus to the heart of cycling.

PREDICTIONS FOR THE 70's

A British rider will finish in the first three in the Tour de France.

A gold medal for British cycling in the Munich Olympics.

A British roadman/time trialist will win the Grand Prix des Nations.

A 'Classic' with support from all the top Continental teams will be staged in Britain with 'live' television coverage for Eurovision.

A coloured rider will win the 'White Hope' sprint at Herne Hill.

A British time trialist/roadman will not win the Grand Prix des Nations.

The World Cycling Championships will be back in Britain by 1976.

Britain will win her first world Cyclo-Cross championship medal.

Two new tracks will be built in Britain.

CHAPTER ONE

'MEXICO '68'

As the shot rang out I was half way across the Anillo Periferico, one of Mexico City's main highways, the scene of the start and finish of the 100 kilometres team time trial. The roads, in readiness for the start, were lined by troops from the Campo Militar Numero Una, the entrance not a hundred yards from where I stood. Recalling the riots just a week or so earlier when a number of students were shot, I got ready to hit the deck!

Half-turning to where the staccato report had emanated I saw a man falling to the ground. For a moment I thought he had been shot dead. I then saw and heard the revolver in his right hand, the muzzle in his mouth, fire again, blowing off the back of his head.

It was a lovely sunny morning, I had enjoyed my breakfast and, even though it was obvious that the man, in civilian clothes, had killed himself, I looked warily around for a few seconds before making tracks to a slightly safer and less sickening spot than the twenty yards range I held at that moment.

I went over and chatted to the British team of Roy Cromack, Peter Smith, John Watson and John Bettinson who were seated about fifty yards away from the disaster. Eddie Soens was giving them his usual excellent massage treatment and I was loath to mention the nasty incident in case it upset them before the off. British team Manager, Maurice Cumberworth, had seen the body and he, too, was complaining about having eaten too much for breakfast!

Most of the journalists in the Press Stand knew nothing of the occurrence a hundred yards away, having probably been busy grabbing a good seat. I managed to squeeze myself in near Mike Hughes of U.P.I. and there were a number of raised

13

eyebrows when I told them of the incident. Some just didn't believe it and one Dutchman reckoned it was a team manager who had just found out the course was nearly four kilometres above the normal distance!

The body lay there for quite a time, soldiers providing a screen until an ambulance arrived. An argument developed then because the ambulance men were not prepared to take him as he was dead, and they drove off in a huff. The human screen decided it had had enough, too, and they moved off, covering the unpleasant sight with newspapers. I did not see the eventual removal but was told a van from the mortuary came and collected the body about three-quarters of an hour after the poor man took his own life.

Why he did it I do not know. There were some thoughts that he had done it in protest against the student killings, the troops having fired on them coming from the Camp nearby. Whatever the case it was just another suicide as far as the papers were concerned next day, the news being limited to a small paragraph and giving no information as to the 'whys' or 'wherefores'.

The tragic incident disappeared from my mind as the team time trial, with thirty nations competing, began. The route took them out to the Queretaro Highway junction, north of the city, where they turned for the inward half to home with quite a number of hills to upset their rhythm.

The course was more than the regulation distance, the officials giving in to complaints by several team managers, to inform everyone it was 51 kilometres to the turn but most people reckoned it was a bit further than that.

Everyone was out to see the famous Swedish Pettersson brothers, Gosta, Erik, Sture and Tomas who had won this event in the world championships in 1967 after taking the bronze medal in the Tokyo Olympics. They were the favourites and went off last, the field leaving at four minute intervals.

By the time they departed the times were coming in for the half distance, Holland, gold medallists in Tokyo, were fastest in 1 hr 3 mins 11 secs with Italy, who took the silver in Japan, just 39 secs behind them. Great Britain, not expected to do a brilliant ride, not in my book anyway, took the turn in 1 hr 7 mins 9 secs, a respectable time but nothing to shout about.

Always the optimist I figured if they could improve slightly they might manage sixth place but they didn't, slumping on the return trip to record 2 hrs 16 mins 38 secs, finishing in eleventh place. Not bad really out of thirty nations. Not bad? A downright disgrace when one considers that Britain is supposed to be a time trialling country. After all, that is the section of cycling sport we have been brought up on over the past sixty odd years until road racing was at last brought in. (See Chapter 12.)

No disrespects to Bettinson, Cromack, Smith and Watson, they did their best which was far from good enough. As pure roadmen, only Bettinson perhaps filled the bill but the other three were beginning to show in road races which was something better than had happened on other occasions when only time trialists were chosen.

Smith had shown well on the road that season, his eighth place in Brno in the 'worlds' the following year proving that and he will get better as time goes on. Incidentally, he and Watson rode with Doug Dailey and Martyn Roach in the team time trial in Brno and did 2 hrs 11 mins 28 secs and took tenth place, knocked out of ninth position by eight-tenths of a second by the French. Admittedly it was over a slightly shorter course but it was a reasonable performance. Reasonable? The Pettersson brothers who won it were ten minutes faster!

Some day we are going to forget about time trials and just regard them as part of the road racing scene. For the team time trial we have to put in four top roadmen, even if we take them out of the road team itself in a world championship to save our faces from the Continental ridicule.

They laugh at our talk of time trials and clutch their ribs at the idea of 12 hour events. So you have good time trialists, they say. Why do they not compete in the Grand Prix des Nations? Over to the R.T.T.C., who would get far more

15

publicity out of that than any British Best All-Rounder Competition.

Sorry about the sudden deviation but that's the way it grabs me, sometimes. Back to the action of Mexico with the Dutch, off second, finishing in 2 hrs 7 mins 49 secs, only fractionally slower on the return leg. They lost Fedor Den Hertog in the last six miles with a puncture and wisely refused to wait for him.

The Dutch team comprised Den Hertog, Rini Pijnen, Jan Krekels and Joop Zoetemelk. If you have any doubts about their being roadmen a quick breakdown gives us Den Hertog, Dutch road champion that year and later to win the Milk Race (see Chapter 19). Pijnen won the Scottish Milk Race and took the bronze medal in the world amateur road title in 1967. Zoetemelk, second in the Dutch championships behind Den Hertog went on to win the Tour de L'Avenir in 1969 and Jan Krekels was already known in Britain, having won the Harp Lager Grand Prix.

Those four men deserved a medal just for sitting around and waiting for about two hours before they knew they had won or got the silver. Sweden were blasting their way around the course and had passed the halfway mark a second faster than the Dutchmen.

On the return trip Tomas punctured and there was a mix-up as they waited for a service vehicle and lost nearly a minute's valuable time. I do not think that puncture would have made any difference at all, the Petterssons finished with 2 hrs 9 mins 26 secs to take second place from Italy but trailing the magnificent Dutch quartet by over one and a half minutes.

So the favourites were beaten, an almost incredible thing for the Swedes went on to collect the gold medals for this event in the world championships in 1968 and 1969. But Munich 1972 is too far away and Gosta, Erik, Sture and Tomas will never possess an Olympic gold to match their twelve other gold medals which have gone to a remarkable Swedish cycling family.

The track events on the beautifully constructed 333 metre

wooden bowl, designed by that great track architect, Herbert Schurman were remarkable for the times above all other things. Here, in the rarer atmosphere, the times went down to reach levels which could never be expected to be beaten again, unless they were achieved at a similar altitude.

Pierre Trentin produced an almost incredible 1 min 3.91 secs for the kilometre, collapsing after his ride and requiring oxygen before he could mount the rostrum to take the gold medal. The French really hit the gold standard on the Mexico track with Trentin taking another gold in the tandem event with Morelon, who himself gained the sprint gold medal. The biggest upset was an unknown rider, Daniel Rebillard, who emerged from nowhere to win the 4,000 metres pursuit.

There were some pretty fantastic times but nothing for Britain who just do not seem to be able to reach a high enough standard on the track these days. Young Ian Hallam rode well but failed to qualify for the individual pursuit although he could be a force in later years.

Most of Britain's hopes lay in the Olympic Road Race which had the same start and finish point as the team time trial. Les West, Billy Bilsland, Brian Jolly and Dave Rollinson were the men with the main chance with West outstanding but a puncture put paid to him on the very first lap.

A break had gone on the big climb and West was with it as they reached the summit when the Stoke man had his moment of disaster. The service vehicles were not there, they were at the bottom of the climb with the rear, struggling group of Congolese, Japanese and all the other no-hopers. West fretted and fumed for all of two minutes before he got a spare wheel and by then it was too late.

Jolly tried to reach the leaders and he suffered the same fate with the same problem of not getting a wheel quick enough. Bilsland had similar misfortunes but like a good Scot, although way down, ploughed his way alone round the course, thinking, no doubt, of all the money spent getting him there and he was going to make the most of it!

Poor West. He sat in the team pits so dejected that no one

spoke to him for some time for fear he would burst into tears. I remember looking at him alongside a sympathetic Chris Brasher and Clement Freud, all of us remarking upon the fact that he was sitting on a couple of bananas and had never even noticed it in his misery.

So the interest centred on the race itself which was a real cracker. Pierfranco Vianelli of Italy won it, after being a member of the team time trial squad that took the bronze. Vianelli broke away from the Dane, Lief Mortensen, with about six miles to go to take the gold but, while Mortensen plodded in alone for the silver, a truly superb piece of riding was going on behind them.

As they began the last ten mile lap the two leaders were well clear of a small chasing group. From these vain pursuiters came Gosta Pettersson with another wonderful display of riding. As the last miles came and went he took handfuls of seconds out of the two ahead, and had there been another lap I am sure he would have made that Olympic gold instead of gaining just another bronze.

Mortensen, too, was a little unlucky for he had made most of the running and was away alone for a time, being joined by Vianelli before the last lap. The Dane got his revenge in Brno the following year when he pedalled away from the leading group to win the amateur world title in the grandest possible manner – alone.

Above all, I shall remember Mexico for the wonderful, sporting crowds. Well-informed, they usually supported the underdogs if there were no particular favourites to cheer. The biggest surprise was to hear from the packed terraces around the Velodromo the chant of 'England, England' and even 'Liv-er-pool, Liv-er-pool' not just for the British but, for anyone they fancied, whatever their nationality!

CHAPTER TWO

TOUR WINS FOR BRITAIN

Towards the latter end of the Sixties the foreign victories in the Tour of Britain Milk Race have increased with wins for Poland in 1966, Sweden in 1968, through Gosta Pettersson, and in 1969 with Dutchman, Fedor Den Hertog.

Before that time one had to go back to 1962 when another Pole, Eugen Pokorny, took the final yellow jersey but, between times, there were some excellent British wins quite apart from those two very fine successes by Les West (see Chapter 4).

Billy Holmes, the Yorkshireman with a wide grin and as tough as old boots, proved a worthy and popular winner in 1961 after being overshadowed by Bill Bradley, his England team mate, in the previous year.

Holmes, second in 1960 and relegated to the Northern team, never won a stage that year but took overall victory with a mere three minute advantage over Spaniard Juan Uribezubia. Nicknamed 'Scoobie-Doobie' by the race followers, this tall, blond Spanish rider earned himself the 'Most Meritorious' award with some great racing, particularly in the mountains.

It was in the mountains that Holmes very nearly lost the race, puncturing with only 15 miles to go after the descent of the Devil's Staircase, en route to Aberystwyth to complete the 7th stage.

His strong Northern team, took overall victory in that department but did not assist him greatly at that point but a service car was close to hand and Holmes was able to rejoin the leading group. Among that breakaway was a man almost unheard of until he won the first stage that year, from Blackpool to Nottingham. His name was Peter Chisman and as a member of Holmes' team, he should have perhaps helped but went on to win the stage that day with Holmes close behind.

Arguments will still rage as to whether or not the tall, well-built young man from Houghton le Spring, did the gentlemanly thing in taking the stage from his leader and many will retain the thought that it was a selfish act. I think Chisman did the right thing because it was difficult in that final sprint to ensure Holmes got to the line first and it was his duty to get victory for the team and keep the winner's time bonus away from anyone else into the bargain.

Holmes hung on to the end, despite the attentions of the Spaniard and while these two and Chisman, who finished fourth overall, were very much the men of the race there was one other rider that needed watching and, for me, was the outstanding man throughout the whole Tour.

This was New Zealander, Warwick Dalton, who finished third overall, won two stages and the Points Classification and he did it without any team support and might have been challenging for the lead itself had he had more luck on a mechanically-troubled day.

He rode for the Southern team, living in London at about that time and, quiet and friendly off the bike he proved a powerful opponent once the race got under way! Oh! for a few more Daltons in British cycling. Such spirit and aggression is so generally lacking in the amateur scene that he was an example to hold up in any discussion or coaching class.

1963 was Chisman's year without any doubt at all and the way he began that Milk Race startled everyone with wins on the opening two stages. But the gap he had opened up through those fine rides began to close as the race swung north-east and one other man's name hung on everyone's lips, Constantin Dumitrescu of Rumania.

This man from behind the Iron Curtain, always distinctively clad in black socks, reduced a deficit of nearly a quarter of an hour to a mere handful of minutes as the race progressed. What might have happened had a Cleethorpes Corporation bus not taken a hand in things, goodness knows!

It was on the eighth stage from Northampton where the Rumanian had taken his first stage the day before. After several breaks had been absorbed the field were together as they swept along the road a few miles from the finish on Cleethorpes promenade. Suddenly, Dumitrescu took off, his lead increasing with every pedal revolution until he was two hundred yards clear and the 'half mile to go' sign looming up. Approaching a 'Y' junction to bear right on to the seafront, the police having stopped traffic coming from the left, he seemed set for victory.

A double-decker bus lumbered into view, its driver not seeing the policeman at the head of the queue of halted traffic and slowly it overtook the stationary line and drove across the road and the path of the oncoming rider. The Rumanian had to apply the brakes to avoid hitting it and, as he slowed to a crawl the bunch were on to him and gratefully swallowed him up!

The tears of rage and frustration wiped away, Dumitrescu went on to win the tenth and eleventh stages, both at Scarborough, one a mountain time trail the other a road race and each one taking place on Oliver's Mount. He narrowed the gap to five minutes but there it ended for a lack of team support eventually told and he had to be content with second place.

But this was Chisman's Tour, a Tour which broke all records for sunshine although it was a day of strong winds when Chisman launched his bid for the first stage win from Blackpool to Nottingham.

Again fate took a hand, this time it was a boat and not a bus for at Warrington, where Chisman was about two minutes up with a group of twelve, the Swing Bridge closed to allow traffic on the Manchester Ship Canal to pass through. The bunch cooled their heels for nearly five minutes and that was that.

With about 90 miles to go and nearly every team represented in the break the seven minutes advantage increased until the Peaks of Derbyshire were reached. Eleven minutes clear the escape fell to pieces as they turned and wilted under the full force of the gale.

Chisman forged ahead, quickly gaining three minutes at the summit of the first climb. The break was made and although he tired as he entered the outskirts of Nottingham, Chisman rode on to the Forest Recreation Ground with the cheers of ten thousand ringing in his ears, nearly ten minutes clear of the next rider to finish.

The stage to Cheltenham the next day, which he again won easily, further improved his position, putting him over 12 minutes clear of the next rider, another Rumanian, Gabriel Moiceanu, who crashed and retired the next day.

So 'Chis' scored a great and memorable win, coming in at Blackpool having retained the yellow jersey from start to finish, only the second rider to do so up to that time, Bill Bradley being the first in 1959.

In the following year, 1964, it was another British win and a popular one too, with Leeds rider, Arthur Metcalfe taking the major honours which included the Points Classification, second in the King of the Mountains and leading the England squad to the team race victory.

It was a hard 1,400 miles with bad weather over most of the fortnight's racing and such was the measure of the England team's strength that they finished with four riders in the first seven although they only won three stages. For the record they were Colin Lewis, Chisman and Metcalfe himself with Terry West being the other member of the party to end the race in the top seven.

Metcalfe's victory on the third stage which gave him the jersey for the rest of the race, was typical of this hard, raw-boned Yorkshireman. Pouring with rain right from the Aberystwyth start with 120 miles to Cardiff and the attacks began on the Abergeswyn Mountain road, where the Spaniards provided the animation.

It was on the third climb of the day after a big regrouping that Metcalfe attacked and went clear with about 70 miles to go. He was unstoppable that day and a brilliant solo performance brought him the win that he so richly deserved.

His closest enemy was an ebullient Spaniard, Vicente Lopez Carril, who won the King of the Mountains and provided the England team with a load of worry right to the end particularly on the 12th stage with only a few minutes separating the two top men.

It was the usual tough route from Newcastle to Morecambe and everything went crazy on the third climb of the day when Carril attacked, leaping out of the saddle and up the hill like a mountain goat. Terry West and Lewis went after him for there were time bonuses to contend with on the primes, as Derek Hepple brought up race leader Metcalfe.

Mike Cowley, riding for the Britannia team and showing well with two stage wins, tacked on to them when, out of the blue, Metcalfe punctured. John Clarey, another watchful member of the England squad was immediately to hand to provide his machine and the yellow jersey lost no time.

Carril was caught and guarded for the rest of the stage and on the final day he rode part of the way in the bunch with his arm round Metcalfe. What a likeable character he was and what an ovation he received at the final race banquet when he collected his second place prize.

CHAPTER THREE

RUSSIA IN BRITAIN

Ever since the world championships accepted women's racing in 1958 there has been a strong move by Russia to get women's cycling included in the Olympic Games.

A glance at the record books will soon provide a reason. Russians have taken 17 gold medals out of a possible 36 since the competition began to say nothing of 35 silver and bronze medals. If it had not been for Mrs Beryl Burton (see Chapter 5) who took seven golds herself and the Belgian, Yvonne Reynders who also collected the same number of gold medals in the three events for women, there would have been an even greater measure of superiority.

It is always difficult to understand the Russian outlook on sport. They refuse to recognise professionals and yet the system they adopt to aid and train their athletes in many different sports, is just as professional, if not better than the treatment and assistance given to the best paid sportsmen and women in the Western world.

Bearing in mind that their competitors rarely move into the open sporting world unless they have a good chance of victory, it was with keen interest that I travelled to see the then amateur Vaux Grand Prix in 1965. The USSR had accepted the invitation to race in this event which has now become probably the finest classic race in the British professional calendar.

It is certainly one of the hardest races in Britain, the course taking in three big climbs of the Durham Moors on each of four laps of a circuit based on the village of Wolsingham. Excellent police co-operation, the best in the country for many years, together with really efficient organisation, has helped to build everything up to this first-class standard.

After the race became a professional event in 1967, thanks

again to the farsightedness of the sponsors, Vaux Breweries, the award of 'Organiser of the Year' went to Tom Rennoldson, of the Houghton Cycling Club, for his tremendous work on the race. This is an award presented annually by the British Professional Association and its recipient gains the title only through the votes of the riders.

Russia came to County Durham and won. Alexander Sabko took the Vaux Gold Tankard while Yuri Pominov won the King of the Mountains title. They could not pull off the team victory though, that went to France who, with Belgium, were the other overseas competing teams.

The Russian victory was not an easy one, Sabko winning only in the final sprint against Jim Leitch of Scotland but their strength in depth was easily seen in the Tour of Britain Milk Race the following year when the USSR came to our shores.

Pominov was one of their team and they finished with three riders in the top five overall places. Their best man, Stanislav Shepel, finished second, only 12 secs behind Josef Gawliczek of Poland and it was with the Poles that they had their big battle.

They did not win many stages but with Shepel in second position, Pominov, fourth and Victor Tkachenko fifth, the team race was theirs by 17 mins. It was a triumph of team work and, I suspect, mainly to ensure that the magic letters 'USSR' were at the top of the team classification, Gawliczek was not attacked hard enough. A 12 secs deficit in a road race is not difficult to beat when there is a strong team together on the road. Perhaps I am being unkind to the Poles and their leader or even a little unjust to the Russians but the latter nation's conduct in later Tours does tend to make one think that it was the team race that interested them most.

In the 1967 Milk Race they took the team race again but with Les West in command at the front they really would have had to fight hard for overall victory. As it was they rode very well but did not manage to wrest the team leadership from Poland until the penultimate stage.

It was this mountainous ride from Carlisle to Morecambe

that produced a big surprise and a man who will always be remembered by the riders and officials that year, Victor Sukhorutchenkov. Perhaps it was fitting that the man with the longest name should win the longest stage, 119 miles, but it was the method he employed that endeared him to everyone. Nicknamed, 'Super-whooping cough' the solidly built Russian took off alone in the cobbled streets of Alston on the second climb of the day with 90 miles to Morecambe and he was not seen again by the field.

Sukhorutchenkov finished five minutes up on the next rider and his wonderful performance that day gave Russia the team lead by those five minutes which they kept to the end. This was a gamble which paid off. I do not think the Russians were as strong that year as in 1966 but they still achieved what they set out to do in the face of strong opposition from Italy, Poland, France and Switzerland as well as three home teams.

It was a different story in 1968 when the formidable Swedish rider Gosta Pettersson led the race throughout, right from the opening evening time trial on Brighton seafront. This quiet, sad-faced but brilliant rider was never really challenged for the jersey and the race became a procession.

It was probably the most boring Tour I have been on and yet there was always the possibility that someone could wipe off the complacent look on the faces of the four Pettersson brothers who held the team lead for Sweden, too.

Russia, Poland, Holland and Denmark were the other continental teams and the old adversaries, Russia and Poland were strangely quiet during the opening stages. After the fifth stage, Victor Sokolov of Russia moved into second overall place behind big brother Gosta but not in a challenging position as he was six minutes down.

It was felt then that the Russians would attack in an attempt to get Sokolov nearer the yellow jersey but they were more content to move other riders further up the table. Russia took the team lead at Stoke, mid-way through the race after they had managed to get two men with the break which, unusually, did not contain any Swedes.

Sokolov should have been one of them but he was still in the main field. Had he been there it might have proved a very different race. As it was, on that stage seven, a young and unknown British rider, Sid Barras, scored his second stage win of the Tour and immediately became Stoke's public enemy number one!

Les West was in the breakaway and, coming into his home town with the large crowd roaring him on, Barras pipped him to the line easily and West had to wait until Berwick, four days later, before he could get his stage win.

Russia had what they wanted, the team lead, which they retained despite losing the team time trial from Hull to Bridlington to the Swedes. As the race wound its way up to the north-east and turned across to the opposite coast they sat tight and defended it. Sokolov stayed with Pettersson or was it the other way round? Whatever the case I am sure that if Russia had attacked a number of other teams would have joined in but they seemed content.

It was a poor race and I blame the Russians for helping to make it so. They got their only stage win at Hull on the ninth day when Yuri Polupanov took the honours and the yellow jersey of Pettersson G., with monotonous regularity, marked, watched and went with everything that moved off the front. He was a worthy winner, no doubt of that, but I would have liked to have seen a challenge, to have seen how Pettersson would have responded to it had things been difficult.

But it never worked out that way and he and the Russians rode into Blackpool for their respective victories. I cannot recall a less popular winner than the tall, untalkative Swede. He rarely smiled and seemed to find it difficult to even acknowledge the applause of the crowds each day as he donned a fresh yellow jersey.

So Russia took their third successive team victory in as many years but there was to be a big surprise in store for them in 1969, when they came a cropper in no uncertain manner. They won only one stage in that Tour, the team time trial, and finished fourth in the team race, unable to get a rider in the first ten overall.

They had sent a good but apparently inexperienced squad and the challenge was much stronger and far harder than had been the case in the previous year and the story of their downfall can be read about in Chapter 19.

CHAPTER FOUR

WAY OUT WEST

Les West is probably one of the finest natural bike riders the world has ever known. He is also his own worst enemy and is as unpredictable as the British weather.

Twice winner of the Tour of Britain Milk Race, twice amateur champion, second in the world amateur road championship in 1966, former British amateur hour record holder and winner of countless events in Britain, both amateur and professional, over a number of years, he could still have been better.

Head and shoulders above the majority of riders in Britain and certainly equal to many on the Continent West, with proper advice and training, might well have been a top professional abroad. He had his opportunity after the Nurburgring in 1966 where he produced that wonderful ride to take Britain's first medal in the road title event for amateurs for over forty years.

His second place then, being beaten by Dutchman Eef Dolman by just two lengths at the line, was a formidable achievement and everyone that saw his performance that day knew they were watching a real bike rider.

Offers of contracts for the big teams came in but after a lot of discussion, argument and chit-chat, our Westey stayed at home, an amateur at heart then and perhaps not unwisely, his sights set on the Olympic Games two years later.

If he had gone to 'the other side' I am sure he would have been a success as would so many other top riders bred in this country. Unfortunately he did not want to take the plunge and, like those other potential stars, remained to produce rides that would have met with equal success abroad where cycling really counts.

It is useless to say that cycling means something in this country except to the enthusiasts and race followers. The British public, swamped by soccer, cricket, rugby and boxing day after day, with some occasional mention of athletics and swimming, just do not learn enough about the sport although I am sure quite a lot would enjoy it if they did.

There are few folk at home with the experience to train up and coming riders and it has been men like West who have managed to reach the top through their own ability and not as a result of the teachings of eminent men in Continental cycling.

The situation is improving though but there is a lot of ground to be covered before the British Cycling Federation can produce good team managers, still few and far between, to not only look after a team, but give them a chance of victory, too.

Chas Messenger was one, helping West to his silver medal in 1966 and gaining the gold with Graham Webb in Holland in 1967. But Messenger also seemed his own worst enemy and had to tell people what he thought, and so, the following year, no Chas, which is another story.

Cruel luck robbed West of the chance of an Olympic medal in Mexico (see Chapter 1) when he punctured on the first lap of the road race and had to wait nearly two minutes for a wheel. The greatest compliment he could be paid came from foreign team managers who told their riders, 'Watch West'. On days when he didn't win he would grumble in that slightly Black Countryish accent, 'I was cramping oop' or 'They followed me ivrywheyre'.

Despite his two excellent amateur title wins it was perhaps in the Tour of Britain, the Milk Race, where he really reigned supreme, his victory in 1967 being a classic example of his prowess and strength.

Heading the Great Britain team that year he steam-rollered his way to a splendid victory over a good-class field containing Russians, Poles, French and Italians, winning by the large margin of 17 mins 47 secs with an almost unknown rider then, David Rollinson, riding for the Provinces team, in second overall place.

West won three stages including the gruelling mountain time trial up the Great Orme at Llandudno, this performance coming the day after he had taken the victor's laurel wreath for the 5th stage from Aberystwyth to the scene of his next triumph.

He was completely unstoppable, either on the flat or in the mountains, the measure of his tremendous ability seemed to leave everyone else floundering in his wake.

One wonders what might have happened in 1966 but for one of those incidents that could only occur in Britain. West was riding well in the Tour and in a good position after winning a stage when the race reached Swindon at the halfway mark of the event.

It was a split stage that day, Swindon to Banbury, 58 miles, with a team trial of 28 miles in the afternoon from Banbury to Coventry. No one was expecting any great developments in that short morning run but on the outskirts of Cirencester after only 14 miles the race was given up as lost by a number of men.

There was action at the front with the then race leader Stanislav Shepel (USSR), his nearest rival and King of the Mountains leader, Josef Gawliczek (Poland) and several others on the attack. Hugh Porter, riding for the Midlands, the same team as West, was the Points leader and also riding well when the officials stopped the race.

Shepel, Gawliczek, Peter Abt of Switzerland, Surminski of Poland and several others had just broken away and were about 300 yards up the road when it happened. The bunch were echeloned from gutter to gutter and, as was usual, with little or no police escort, the officials got in a tizzy.

The peleton was stopped for almost a minute as the escape, marvelling in its good fortune, did the best they could do to improve their happy situation. The best they did was over eight minutes at the line and the bottom had fallen out of the race for West, Porter and a number of others.

Porter eventually lost the Points Classification by just two points to Poland's 'Fred' Surminski. (He was an old hand on

31

the Milk Race and Fred seemed better than the mouthful of Franticzek every time!)

West finished in 6th overall place, four of the men in front of him being in that break that went before the bunch were halted. He was just over eleven minutes down on the winner, Gawliczek, who took the honours in the closest ever finish, being 12 secs clear of the Russian Shepel at Blackpool.

West's name is down in the record books for the Vaux classic and the Isle of Man amateur International as well as that great opening race of the season, the Harp Lager International and, on reflection, there is very little this man has not won or certainly come very close to doing so.

I sometimes wonder how many more races he would have won, including the amateur title in 1968, if he had had a sprint. No disrespects to that cheeky chappie from Liverpool, Peter Matthews, who did win it that year but Les had made most of the running and lost the chance of being the first rider to take the British amateur road title three times by about a length.

West turned professional for Holdsworth Cycles in 1969 and began a new career, closely watched by his faithful followers. The professional class had only been going for three years when he joined their ranks and it did not take him long to score his first win.

This came in the Mackeson three day event on the Isle of Wight, moved there from Bournemouth by the sponsors because of moderate organisation and a lack of assistance by the police. The Island was not much better that year, the authorities there showing little appreciation of what was going on and the same sort of mediocre co-operation from the police.

The riders put on a good show as one had come to expect from the professionals and those who braved the cold weather thoroughly enjoyed themselves in seeing West's first victory in the paid ranks.

West won the first stage with a typical lone effort, finishing well clear of the field to take a lead which he never relinquished. In the time trial stage over 15 miles the following day he took

Sture, Gosta, Tomas and Erik (*left to right*), the famous Swedish Pettersson brothers who have won the world 100 km team trial event three times. Here in Mexico City they were on their way to an Olympic silver despite their silk jerseys and lack of socks to cut down wind resistance and lighten the load. *See* Chapter One

Race Leader of the 1961 Tour of Britain, Bill Holmes (*left*) leads one of his keenest rivals in the event, Warwick Dalton of New Zealand. *See* Chapter Two

Traffic and the unhelpful British police leave the Tour of Britain riders little alternative but to get through as best they can. Fortunately police assistance has improved since this picture was taken in the mid-sixties.
See Chapters Two and Three

The wet Buckinghamshire lanes. The Harp Lager International field led by two British stalwarts, Les West (*left*) and the late Peter Buckley (*right*).
See Chapter Four

second place, losing to that formidable performer, Colin Lewis, but easily kept his leader's jersey despite many attacks.

He will win many more races but I cannot remember him better than at the moment of flight at the Nurbürgring in 1966. On that flat finishing section of road as the last lap began West shook off the attentions of a small group and just showed them his rear wheel.

That he was eventually caught by Dolman and beaten in that final sprint was no disgrace for he made his mark in no uncertain manner and it would be no surprise to me to see Leslie West, Great Britain, taking a classic victory or even a medal in a world championship in the years he still has before him.

CHAPTER FIVE

'TAILOR-MADE FOR BURTON'

Women on racing cycles? It's all a bit of a joke really and I know I am not alone for there are many others who share this view. Those that do not are all the women competitors and to name one person in particular, Mrs Eileen Gray, of the women's Cycle Racing Association and British Women's Team Manager for countless occasions.

It is all rather undignified and slow, especially on the track and I cannot think what might have happened to British racing on the distaff side had it not been for one graceful and certainly far from slow Beryl Burton.

Mrs Beryl Burton won seven world titles between 1959 and 1967, two of them on the road and five in the 3,000 metres pursuit. She also took four silver and one bronze medal in world competition and her record in Britain is almost impossible to repeat.

Not only has she taken just about every British women's title since she began racing but she has even beaten the men as well. Beryl seemed to go faster as she grew older for in 1967 she produced a fantastic ride in the Otley 12 hour event, covering an almost unbelievable 277.2 miles in that time.

She beat the men almost out of sight that day on the Yorkshire roads she knows so well, the nearest to her being Mike McNamara of the Rockingham Cycling Club with 276.8 miles. This, for him, was a new competition record but he could hardly have had much satisfaction from it after being beaten by a woman!

In the following year Mrs Burton achieved another of her great ambitions, to get inside four hours for the hundred miles. On the Essex roads, with a slight drizzle dampening everything

34

but her truly great spirit and ability she romped home with another superb ride in 3 hrs 55 mins 5 secs.

During the Sixties she has completely dominated the women's racing scene, holding records for just about any and every distance you care to mention. Records, events, Best All-Rounder titles, they have all fallen to this quite amazing Yorkshire woman.

In 1969 she rode in a Ladies' 24 hour event, run in conjunction with the men's National championship over that distance. She was firmly in the lead at the halfway distance and, after 345 miles was heading the leading male rider by 23 minutes.

Terrible luck was to befall her then. A knee, perhaps an old injury aggravated by her long ride, began to swell and her hopes of winning this event diminished as the pain and swelling continued. Soon after that 345 mile point she had to stop and, although remounting and bravely continuing she had to stop once more.

Twelve miles after that first stop Roy Cromack swept by to go on to win the title and set a record at the same time, 507 miles in 24 hours. A formidable ride and one which I do not think even Beryl could have beaten had she been completely fit but one never knows when dealing with this quite remarkable woman.

Had she not been a time-trialist I think she might well have won more world titles, particularly on the road. It was there that her great strength was the key to success, a strength one must admit, built up by the pressures of those time trials in Britain.

But she lacked a sudden turn of speed, the quick jump forward and the switch across the road to break clear of one's opponents. Had she been blessed with such an advantage or had been able to learn the technique she could have taken the women's title every year without difficulty.

On the track she was supreme in the 3,000 metres pursuit event, her five titles in that competition making it fairly obvious and yet, I think, she could still have done better had she concentrated more on short distances instead of battling her way round Britain's roads in time trials of a hundred miles and even 12 hours.

This was no way to train for a 3,000 metres event or, for that matter, for a road race of never more than 45 miles. But how can one criticise a world champion of such repute? Surely she should know best but I suspect she was as equally concerned with winning at home as she was abroad.

I was privileged to see her last gold medal ride – I say her last but one never knows with Beryl! It was in Holland in 1967 when twelve nations lined up for the start of the women's road race over four laps of the circuit at Heerlen, just about 33 miles in total.

On the climb at the village of Ubachsberg on the second lap, Beryl broke away with the Russian, Zadorozhnaya. As they went over the top Mrs Burton put her gear into its biggest notch, accelerated and rode away. For a few hundred yards there was little in it and, for a time, it was thought the Russian would bring her back.

She did not. Beryl was away and it was now only a question of how much time she would win by. Mrs Burton continued to draw away from the Russian girl who, creditably, stuck to her guns and took the silver medal, nearly two mins behind her while the bunch came in almost six mins in arrears.

'BB' helped Britain to a double never before achieved in cycling that day. Graham Webb won the amateur road race later to gain two golds from the two events. Those two great rides together with Porter's silver on the track, were called by one Continental journalist, 'The revenge of Tom Simpson', Britain's great man of cycling having died only six weeks earlier.

We shall see Beryl riding in the Seventies I am sure but it is likely to be another Burton who will wipe the floor with the opposition, Beryl's daughter, Denise.

CHAPTER SIX

'SILVER IN AMSTERDAM – GOLD IN ROME'

Hugh Porter has been a roadman-pursuiter of high quality in Britain for a number of years, his bronze medal in the world amateur pursuit in 1963 testifying to his ability and the Commonwealth Games gold medal in 1966 was further proof of his strength and class.

But it was not until 1967 when Porter had turned professional that he was thought to have any chance of a medal in the world championships that year. On the new Leicester track Porter won the British pro title with the sort of riding that made everyone gasp with astonishment. I recall Dutchman Charles Ruys, one of the great characters in British cycling about that time, checking his watch after Porter's ride and exclaiming to me excitedly, 'Man, that was a world class piece of riding.'

It certainly was for Porter had recorded 6 mins 14 secs for the 5,000 metres, a time which could earn him a medal in Amsterdam a few weeks later. It was obvious that he could do a better time since the weather was cold and windy that day in Leicester and cycling held its breath and waited for the worlds.

In Amsterdam's Olympic Stadium we did not have to wait long. Porter qualified with the second fastest time, 6 mins 11.91 secs with the danger man to his title hopes, the big Dutchman, Tiemen Groen, taking the top placing with a time less than a second quicker than the Wolverhampton man.

One big surprise was that the Belgian, Ferdy Bracke, who took the title in 1965, was the slowest qualifier and he eventually departed from the competition at that point, stating that he was ill and not contesting the event further.

The ninth placed man in the qualifying round was then brought in, Jan Schroeder of Holland but his hopes were slim and Porter easily beat him in the quarter finals by 12 secs.

In the semi-finals the long-legged Midlander remorselessly churned round the track against Italian Giacomo Fornoni with another easy ride and went through to the final, beating his opponent by 9 secs.

Groen was a very different proposition though. He, too, had reached the final without extending himself and he knew he must start fast against Porter who never got under way quickly. Big Hughie did his best but it was just not good enough with the Dutch giant coming home by just under 3 secs, Porter pulling a full second back on the last lap.

So it was a silver medal for Porter in his first world professional pursuit and it was a really excellent achievement and said much for the professional class in Britain who must certainly have helped Porter to increase his speed in all the road events that season. Mind you, Porter was always going faster towards the end of a 4,000 metre ride and, with the strength there, he still had a bit more to give for that extra 1,000 metres.

That medal gave the Wolverhampton man quite a bit of confidence for he went on to gain the famous winter track pursuiters great honour, the 'Brassard' during the following months in Belgium.

But the all-important place was Rome in 1968 where, with Groen absent from competition, it seemed that Porter would at last gain the gold medal. But nothing is easy and on that first night of the pursuit, right there in the qualifying round over 5,000 metres, trouble and almost disaster, faced the Wolverhampton man.

Porter was called up to ride first with the West German Siegfried Adler on the opposite side of the track. This was the 'time trial' ride, the fastest eight going through to the quarter-finals, with two riders competing on each run.

Both men were ready and almost immediately after the starter's gun had fired Porter, out of the saddle in the home straight, had his hand in the air and slowing after only two or three pedal revolutions. A toe clip had broken, his strap slid off his shoe and a foot had come out. Alec Taylor, the British team manager was quickly on the scene asking for a re-run as Adler continued his ride alone.

The officials conferred and permitted it but it was a very close decision and Britain's best man was lucky not to have been out of the competition even before he had completed the course!

Porter then had to ride last, sitting with the nervous tension building up and having to watch the times come down. It was thought that around 6 mins 12 secs would be a reasonable time and Adler had already finished, being only a second slower than that. The beautifully constructed wooden track was proving fast and the times continued to fall, much to the dismay of the British contingent.

Little Leandro Faggin, cheered to the echo by his compatriots round the track, turned in a fine 6 mins 9.63 secs and then another Italian, Pietro Guerra, got inside that by four tenths of a second. The Dane, Ole Ritter then lowered it still further with a cracking ride of 6 mins 8.26 secs and Porter was coming out to ride last and alone with no one on the other side of the track to serve as pace-maker or target.

The Stadium in utter silence, Porter began his ride, slowly at first and then the steady rhythm, the powerful legs going fast and smooth as he sped round the track. It took the crowd but a few laps to realise they were watching a terrific pursuiter in action. Hunched over the 'bars, only his legs moving, face twisted in a snarl as he gulped the air into his lungs, Porter rode faster and faster round the wooden bowl, keeping the machine beautifully still and right on the pursuiters' line.

The Italians began to cheer now, the cold, still night air broken at first by just a few spasmodic handclaps in various parts of the arena but it grew as the ride went on and it swelled up into a great roar as the last lap began. Holding the bike still on the line, Porter was flying now and there was no stopping him as the crowd's eyes were riveted first on the electric timing clock and then back to this magnificent rider.

The roar reached its climax as the clock stopped, a roar

which could have been heard for many miles. There for all eyes to see was 6 mins 4.72 secs, a truly memorable ride under the most difficult circumstances.

Fastest qualifier Porter should have had no more problems but there was always a nagging fear that Ritter might pull it off in the end. In the quarter-finals it was Adler who met Porter and what terrible luck for the West German who produced his best ever time for the distance and was still trounced after recording 6 mins 7.18 secs.

Goodness knows what Porter might have done that night had he been pushed by Adler. The big Wolverhampton man was in no mood for niceties and, I think, a little cross as a result of a remark made to him by Mrs Eileen Gray, the British Women's team Manager. She had suggested that he was lucky not to have Beryl Burton riding in the event and Porter, always nervous before a big race, appeared to take it completely the wrong way!

Adler had recently set up a record for the hour on the indoor tracks but he was hopelessly out-classed against Porter who snarled his way round the track in the most formidable manner. The roar from the crowd this time turned into an almost incredulous gasp as the British flying machine recorded 6 mins 0.54 secs, the third fastest time ever in the world!

His semi-final ride against Guerra was a much closer affair and had everyone on tip-toe. The Italian started fast, two seconds up after the opening lap and gradually increased it to nearly 4 secs after another two laps. Porter, warming to his task, held him there and the time gap slowly lessened but there was still about 2 secs to make up just after the halfway mark. The Italian crowd were screaming crazily now for Guerra and for one awful moment I thought Porter had left it too late.

But the pace had become too hot for the Italian and he began to go rubbery in the legs as the Wolverhampton express switched on the full power to go ahead and win comfortably by just under 3 secs. The final now against Ritter who had also easily disposed of his opponents in the previous rounds and showing what danger there might be by recording 6 mins 2.72 secs in one of them.

Rain almost stopped the final before it ever began, the down-pour soaking the track just as the events for the evening were due to begin. Two small Fiat cars, with blankets tied to the back, circled the track and succeeded in drying it out after the rain had ended and the two finalists were left with each other and a stiff breeze in the home straight.

As expected, Ritter started fast and held an early lead but never took as much out of Porter as was expected. After two laps the Dane was 2 secs ahead but never increased it after that and the gap got smaller as the race went on. Only five laps gone and Porter was in the lead, a lead which he held and steadily improved to the end to win, after thoroughly demoralising his challenger, by 8 full seconds.

It was a great moment for the British in Rome that night but nothing to compare with the jubilation of Porter himself who had won his first gold medal in the same city as his wife, the former Olympic swimmer, Anita Lonsborough.

The contracts that came with his title gave Porter some hard riding to do on the winter tracks but he rose to the task well, accepting the fact that he had to learn a new trade and, as a result, is very much a better rider than he was even when he took the world title.

CHAPTER SEVEN

'BILLY BILSLAND, BRIAN JOLLY, ALBERT HITCHEN, BARRY HOBAN, ARTHUR METCALFE, COLIN LEWIS, OLD UNCLE BILL LAWRIE AND ALL...'

'Ici la route de la Tour de France. Soixante kilometres d'arrivée, le Brittanique Metcalfe seul en tete, deux minutes d'avance le peleton.'

Those were the words that electrified me as I turned on the radio to listen to the Tour in 1968. What music that made in my ears with all the usual atmospherics and crackle, snap and pop in the background from the commentator's motor-cycle.

Arthur Metcalfe did not stay away that day and eventually retired from the Tour that year after finishing the race in 1967, his first experience of the gruelling test. Metcalfe should have been racing abroad four or five years before that time. Like Holmes, Hitchen and Bradley he could have made the grade but it is useless to seek one's fortune on the Continent after too long at home.

Metcalfe has not retired in many events, he is a hard man, not, I feel, liked generally by the men in the bunch in Britain but, then, one can never be a success and not have any enemies. In all the events Metcalfe has won in Britain his outstanding achievement, apart from his Tour of Britain victory in 1964, was his tremendous double two years later.

Never achieved before and not bettered in the Sixties, Metcalfe won both the British amateur road title and the British Best All-Rounder Competition in 1966. This called for superb riding and it took cycling by surprise and, one hopes, has helped to disprove the argument about time trialists being better than roadmen or vice versa.

In form and on his day there was probably only one other man in Britain to equal him and that was his former amateur international colleague of many occasions, Colin Lewis.

Lewis rode the Tour de France with Metcalfe in those two years, finishing each one. He has taken the British professional road title twice, 1967 and 1968, his ride on the first of those two championship bids being, perhaps, his best.

On a tough, Essex course, Lewis just rode away from the opposition that hot, July Sunday afternoon. I recall following him and watching his face, strained with effort and running with sweat, as he pounded away at the pedals.

Lewis was a member of the British team in the world championships on the Nurbürgring in 1966, a British team that could hardly have been bettered. Les West, Metcalfe, Lewis, Peter Hill, Mike Cowley and Derek Harrison. All of them great names and managed by that stalwart, Chas Messenger, managed in such a manner that all six finished that title race, the only team to do so.

It is worth recording that hot day in the Eiffel Mountains for it was Lewis who showed first, breaking away alone and setting a fast pace. Once caught it was Hill doing the same thing and then it was the turn of West who went on to take the silver (see Chapter 4). All of them deserved praise that day for they were quite the finest team on the road and one can only really measure their success through the efforts of Messenger himself.

I hope it will not be long before Britain can produce another world title team and a manager to match that wonderful line-up.

Albert Hitchen, that tough, speedy Yorkshireman is, as I have said earlier, another man who should have gone abroad at an early age. Twice winner of the British Independent title, Hitchen has taken just about everything in the British calendar at one time or another.

The Merseyside Four Day, the Holyhead, the Tour of the West, London-York, the Harp Lager Grand Prix, you name it, he's won it! Always with seemingly effortless ease Hitchen could be relied upon to produce a professional performance.

When he won the Pro/Independent championships at Chard, Somerset, in 1965, he was out alone for the last lap with a big enough lead to allow him to 'clean up' before the presentation. Over the last few miles, 'King Albert' sat up for a few moments and used his racing cap to wipe the dust and sweat from his face in readiness for the photographers and the kiss from the local Beauty Queen after the finish.

One good Yorkshireman did go to the Continent to seek stiffer competition and the chance of making a name for himself as Tom Simpson had done. This was Barry Hoban who could have stayed and become a top man in the British racing scene but he chose well and his rides abroad have earned him considerable success.

Strangely enough he only won one classic during the Sixties, the Frankfurt Henninger Turm, in 1966, but he has never been far away from the line on many occasions. He might well have done better, too, had he not had to work for the best man of the Mercier-B.P. team, Raymond Poulidor.

Hoban has won four stages in Tours de France, two of them in successive days on the 1969 event. They were of particular satisfaction to him and both showed his remarkable prowess as a roadman-sprinter. His first win in 1969 was at Bordeaux on the track where he had twice before been beaten in Tour stage finishes. That was his happiest victory but the shining face of Hoban, with its ear-splitting grin, was never more elated than on the very next day on stage 19, from Bordeaux to Brive, when he triumphed again.

This time it was a road finish and not a track sprint and again his opposition was four other men. With the confidence of having beaten Dutchman, Ottenbros, no slouch when it comes to a gallop, the Italian, Pietro Guerra and two Frenchmen, Berland and Rigon, on the Bordeaux concrete bowl, he easily put paid to the opposition at Brive.

Again, Guerra was there with Eddy Schutz of Luxembourg and two formidably fast men were with them, Belgian, Joseph Spruyt and Dutchman Eef Dolman, the latter being the man who beat Les West to take the world amateur title in 1966. Hoban timed it well, thrusting his wheel ahead of Dolman at the line and so helped to put quite a lot of money in his pocket during the criteriums that come after the Tour has ended.

Perhaps though his third place in the Liege-Bastogne-Liege classic earlier that season was one of his finest rides. Merckx had broken away with his team mate Victor Van Schil and, although they were well clear there was a big battle for third place.

A group of ten eventually formed, Hoban being one of them and he was left to do much of the work over many miles. Among the sitters-in were Eric Leman, Herman Van Springel, Frans Verbeeck and Roger Swerts, all crafty roadmen sprinters from Belgium. Gimondi was there, too, but Hoban beat them all with a truly magnificent finish for a very well deserved third place and a mention in the record books.

'Knackered' is a rather rude but nonetheless effective word often used by riders to describe their feelings after a bike race and no one I know says it more succinctly than Sheffield's Brian Jolly. Here is a young man who has already earned himself a place in this chapter even at the age of 23 in 1969 when he won the amateur road title.

Jolly had already been to Mexico as a member of the British road team and the amateur title in 1969 was just one of 25 races that he won that year. Three stages in the Milk Race, two stages in the Scottish Milk Race plus overall victory were some of the high-lights of this very forceful rider.

He was a member of the Great Britain squad in the Tour de

l'Avenir, a team which did quite well in this hard, amateur equivalent of the Tour de France. On the day that David Rollinson won the 3rd stage, Jolly took the yellow jersey. Only for a day but it was a great moment nevertheless and the team rode well to finish fourth overall in the team race ahead of Poland, Sweden/Denmark, Czechoslovakia, Mexico, Spain, and Switzerland.

The final stage over the mountains to Clermont Ferrand was won by another up and coming man, Scot, Billy Bilsland who had the best placing of the British team at the end, eighth overall. Bilsland is another excellent rider, probably the best to come out of Scotland since the days of the great Ian Steel.

I remember Bilsland, riding for Great Britain, producing a wonderful solo ride on the penultimate stage of the Tour of Britain Milk Race in 1968. To say that it was pouring with rain that day would be an understatement. It literally fell down over the last 25 miles with Bilsland riding through it all as if it was non-existent to take the stage into Morecambe in fine style.

Here is a good hard Scot who, like Jolly, will be riding professionally in the '70's. I am certain we shall be hearing a lot about them.

I am sure no one will complain if I bring in an Australian among the British names in this chapter. After all he won the British professional road title in 1969 and has graced the boards of the winter tracks all over Europe with some excellent racing.

It is Bill Lawrie, a quiet, tall, good-looking man whose style and ability has won him two Australian Six Day events as well as the British road title and ten mile championship. Bill was almost 35 years of age when he took the Professional title after a most exciting race. Riding for Falcon Cycles I remember there was some confusion after the event as some people were wondering if he was permitted, as an Australian, to take the title.

The British Cycling Federation soon cleared the matter up by saying, 'Yes' and everyone breathed a sigh of relief that this likeable Aussie, who had graced our roads and tracks for some years, could hold on to the title he had so rightfully earned.

There are many other riders in the Sixties but it is just not possible to find room for them all. I can only apologise for not naming more men who have helped to make cycle racing in Britain, more exciting and more colourful over a ten year period which, I for one, enjoyed whole-heartedly. I hope, too, that the Seventies will bring many new faces to entertain us in the same way and help to increase the standards of competition as those men of the Sixties did.

CHAPTER EIGHT

THE RAIN IN SPAIN...

The wettest weather for many years descended on the world cycling championships of 1965 in San Sebastian, the scene of Britain's greatest triumph when Tom Simpson won the professional road title.

The organisation was very patchy but everything brightened up for the small British contingent when Simpson beat the West German, Rudi Altig in the final dash for the line and the memory of that wonderful victory carried everyone through the wet, humid and often crazily arranged track events.

The story of that magnificent moment of British cycling history has been told many times and by a number of people including myself. Even now, though, the recollections of the scene immediately after Tom crossed the line are as clear as if it were last week and not nearly five years ago.

I had just completed a half-screamed, half-sobbed commentary into the microphone for BBC Radio and the next thing to do was an interview. Our own tape-recorder was out of action – soaked by the constant rain over the previous three days, and we borrowed one from the Spanish radio people.

My commentary position, up in the press stand, had no exit on to the road but that way was the shortest route and holding the microphone and dragging the Spanish technician with me, I made tracks for the pits.

There is always sheer chaos after a professional title race has ended and it was no different when I climbed down the 15 feet of wall and barriers and fought my way across the road, my new-found Spanish friend, white under his normal tan, hanging on to the tape recorder several feet behind me.

I got my interview and we forced our way back in time to see the medal presentation on the podium. Simpson, surrounded

Profile view of Hugh Porter in action on the Herne Hill track wearing his 1968 world champion's jersey. *See* Chapter Six

Merckx (*centre*) sprints to the world professional road title, 1967, at Heerlen, Holland. Dutchman Jan Janssen (*right*) was second with Spaniard Ramon Saez (*left*) taking the bronze. *See* Chapter Nine

Barry Hoban winning his
second successive stage of the
1969 Tour de France.
Dutchman Evaert Dolman is
on the left at the end of
the 19th stage at Brive

Simpson acknowledges the
acclaim of the Herne Hill
crowd a few weeks after
winning the world road title
in 1965. *See* Chapters Eight
and Thirteen

by well-wishers, press and radio men from the continent was being pushed and jostled with the large figure of Albert Beurick from Belgium, crying his eyes out in joy, leading the way.

Beurick's ample frontage knocked a route through the packed crowds. I could hear him shouting, 'Champion du Monde!' over the din from thirty yards away, his well-filled stomach thrusting aside police, troops and even metal barriers as he strode towards the podium.

As Simpson mounted the top tier a great roar went up and journalists in the press stand were slapping us on the back, shaking us by the hand and crying alongside us at this very wonderful, moving occasion. There was no national anthems being played that year, I think because Franco didn't approve of the East Germans competing, and they played the 'U.C.I. Hymn' for all medal ceremonies.

As the music blared out on this cold, grey afternoon, the flags drooping and wet, the three medal winners, Simpson in his rainbow jersey and the three bouquets adding a small splash of colour to the drab, raincoated scene, I heard someone singing 'God Save The Queen'.

Looking round I saw dear Kath White, wife of the Daily Express reporter, standing on her seat a few yards away, the tears running down her cheeks, singing at the top of her voice. I tried to join in but my tears had started afresh and I just choked up.

So it was with something of a feeling of anti-climax that I attended the track championships at the Anoeta Stadium in San Sebastian during the next seven days.

The rain still fell down and there were changes, cancellations and alterations to the programme that had everyone hanging around from early morning until late at night. For the press it was a most uncomfortable waiting period as the area set aside, complete with tables, was in the track centre just beyond the finish line – on grass.

There was hardly any grass visible at all, just a sea of muddy water with the tables slowly sinking into it as typewriters were placed on them. Eventually we managed to find some planks of wood, and, rather like duckboards in the trenches in the First World War, we placed them over the morass, walking gingerly to and fro.

I think it got worse as the sun came out for the concrete track reflected the heat and it all began to steam and smell. Cracks about malarial swamps abounded but we put up with it and, with some really exciting racing at times, managed to forget all about it until a foot slipped off the duck boards!

The professional sprint probably provided the most interest with the great Italian Antonio Maspes, seven times world champion, going out to the young, up and coming Belgian, Patrick Sercu, in the quarter finals.

Sercu, Olympic kilometre gold medallist in Tokyo the previous year, was riding his first world championship as a professional. He was a mass of jangling nerves and yet he still produced a fine turn of speed to put paid to the hopes of Maspes.

Out went the Italian in two straight runs, the latter one leaving him sprawled on the track. Maspes tried desperately to hold Sercu out of the last banking and in so doing, pulled his wheel over. The tyre blew and seven gold medals of sprinting got dumped unceremoniously on the concrete, with Sercu, in tears with nerves and delight, crossing the line an easy winner.

The Belgian was beaten in the final by another Italian, Giuseppe Beghetto with Australian Ron Baensch taking the bronze but not before he had put the Stadium in a turmoil of excitement in his quarter-final matches against the 1963 world champion, Sante Giairdoni, who won the Olympic Sprint gold medal for Italy in Rome in 1960.

Baensch, that rough, tough, turbulent character, who usually sets a crowd buzzing as he walks on to the track while the journalists sharpen their pencils and photographers check their cameras, had featured a day earlier on the front page of *The Daily Telegraph*.

It was a different kind of story that I had written and concerned his being arrested by the Spanish Police along with Piet Van Der Touw of Holland, both men receiving quite a beating before they were released.

General Franco, who used San Sebastian as his summer retreat, resting on his yacht moored in the harbour, had been to church and was on his way back when Baensch and the Dutchman returned from a training spin. The police had shut off the road, security was tight for this was the Basque country and no one was being allowed to cross the road until the General had gone.

Baensch and his companion were right opposite their hotel and could not see why they should have to wait and began to walk over the road. Naturally they were prevented from doing so and one can imagine the scene which was then enacted.

Blows were struck on both sides and the upshot of the matter was that Baensch with several policemen hanging on to him, was manhandled into a van along with Van Der Touw, and driven 'downtown'.

Fortunately for them the incident was seen by an Australian amateur, Kevin Crowe, from the window of their hotel, and he reported the facts to the British Consulate. Had he not done so I hate to think what might have happened, certainly it would have been doubtful if Baensch had appeared to ride in the championships on the following day.

The Aussie had taken quite a beating from the police truncheons after being handcuffed, even being struck on the legs when he explained he was riding in the championships. I examined his bruises in the changing rooms and they looked highly painful. He just shrugged them off, expressing his disappointment at not being able to ride against a Spaniard that day!

When the Australian came out to ride, his national professional jersey, all green with the familiar yellow edging, covering most of the bruising, the Stadium was packed to capacity.

General Franco had arrived and was sitting in the home

straight stand under a specially erected canopy in the midst of around two hundred grey-suited secret service men. The rim of the 400 metre track, just above the crowds, was being patrolled by troops armed with machine guns, spaced out every few yards.

News of Baensch's beating must have leaked out for there was a sympathetic cheer as he was called to the line alongside Giairdoni. Franco, dressed in yachting cap and blazer, surveyed the scene, being irreverently described by a colleague as looking like a 'Southend boatman'.

The first run went to Baensch after the Italian had protested, both of them with elbows in each other's ribs and a lot of pushing and leaning around the final banking. The Aussie's popularity was obvious now as the crowd cheered at the announcement which put him one up.

The second run seemed much the same with Baensch thrusting out his arm from the inside position as they came round the curve to prevent Giairdoni pushing him off the track. To a storm of boos, whistles and abuse the Italian's hand went aloft again and this time the over-worked officials gave it to him much to the displeasure of the crowd.

Everything was simmering in the heat as they came up for the decider. After the usual sparring with Giairdoni producing the favourite Italian standstill, forcing the Australian to the front, the sprint exploded into action over the last three hundred yards.

Down the back straight the Italian had still not levelled with Baensch and it was obvious he was not going to do it. Halfway round the banking and with his legs crumpling he reached the Aussie's hip and then threw up his hand again in protest, making out that he had been pushed and moving high up the banking.

The crowd were furious but Baensch, completely calm, easing off as he turned into the finishing straight had plenty of time to look back at his opponent. With a wide grin on his rugged face he gave Giairdoni the well-known sign with two fingers and as the crowd applauded the action he looked up at Franco as he crossed the line and saluted him in a similar manner.

The ecstatic roar of approval which greeted this was amplified only when, after a short discussion by the officials had ended, the announcement came, 'Primero – Baensch!'.

CHAPTER NINE

'MERCKX'

The last few miles of the 1964 Olympic Road Race, the Tokyo roads shining wet and the rain pouring down as three riders approached one of the last corners, holding a lead just big enough to see them to the line.

Dutchman Harry Steevens led the trio round, Eddy Merckx of Belgium just behind him and in close attendance at the rear, Mike Cowley of Great Britain. Steevens slithered and fell leaving the other two men no chance of avoiding him and they were on the ground, the bunch sweeping by and all chance of a medal lost to those three men of courage.

Had Merckx stayed upright he may well have gained his second gold medal within six weeks for, at Sallanches, a small French town at the foot of Mont Blanc, at the beginning of September, Merckx had already taken the world amateur road title.

I saw Merckx win that medal, the rain coming down on the seven and a quarter mile circuit just as it had in Japan, only in France, Merckx was alone at the front. I had heard Tom Simpson talking about him earlier saying that the Belgian boy often called round in Brussels when Simpson was being massaged by his soigneur, Gus Naessens.

Naessens was full of the lad it seemed, and encouraged him to ask questions which Tom usually answered. It was probably a case of being a good listener for, as well as Tom, Vin Denson sometimes attended.

If there had been betting on that amateur title race the odds would have been at least 100–1 with the 130 strong field and Gus Naessens would have made himself a lot of money for he tipped Merckx to win well before the event.

Just eighteen years of age that June, Merckx took the world

title in the same way that he has since dominated many races – alone at the front. The win was perhaps a little fortunate for he was with a small group with about three laps left and the gap closing all the time.

Merckx, sensing that they could get caught, went off with just under two laps left. The others were snaffled up by an enormous bunch who, having caught the break, sat up and waited for the sprint, not realising that one man was ahead of them!

This fact became quite evident when the massed gallop for the line took place. Willy Planckaert of Belgium got there first and immediately flung up his hands to the skies, thinking he had won the world title!

Merckx turned professional the following year for Peugeot-B.P., joining Simpson and in the next two years built up quite a reputation for himself. The result of this was a number of hints in the press abroad about arguments between him and Simpson and it flared into life in the Paris-Nice stage race in 1967.

The rapidly improving Belgian had only nine wins in the 1965 season, none of them great ones, but in the following year he won 19 events including the Italian classic, Milan-San Remo. So he came to Paris-Nice with an ever-growing stature still in the team where Tom Simpson was the top man.

Simpson won Paris-Nice that year and there were stories all over the Continental papers about a rift between these two great riders. No one was now prepared to believe they were friends until Simpson set up Milan-San Remo for Merckx a few days later.

That they were good friends was evidenced by the Belgian's distress when Simpson died on the Tour de France later that year. I wonder how many of the several thousand at the little Parish church at Harworth recognised Eddy Merckx as he came to pay his last respects?

Off the bike, Merckx is a quiet man by nature, but he was unusually silent that day. I looked at him occasionally, just at the end of the pew in front of mine, during the service as he prayed and cried along with the rest of us. I thought then how difficult it was to see the ruthlessness and the strength of this apparently mild, well-mannered man as he knelt there.

After taking the San Remo classic for the second successive year, beating incidentally the record time for the race previously held by Simpson in 1964, Merckx went on record 26 wins in the season.

He won Ghent-Wevelgem, the Flêche Wallonne, the Baracchi Trophy for the second time, and most important of all, he took the world professional road title in one of the most thrilling finishes for many years.

The break had gone early on the eight mile circuit around Heerlen in Holland, quite close to the German border, and it stayed away all day. After about ten laps, Dutchman, Jan Janssen, broke away from the main pack in pursuit, eventually bridging a gap of nearly three minutes to join the leaders. His progress around the circuit could be heard for miles as his fellow countrymen cheered him to the echo and, just as he was about to make contact, there was Bob Addy of the Great Britain team, coming off the back of the break with his legs wilting under the constant pressure.

Janssen is no slouch when it comes to a sprint and with the Italian, Gianni Motta, there too, all was set for a tremendous finish. Merckx got it by little more than a tyre's width from Janssen with Motta surprisingly out of it and the Spaniard, Ramon Saez, who rode the Tour of Britain in 1964, taking the bronze medal.

Merckx was made. Within the space of four years and still only 21 years old, he had taken both the professional and amateur world titles. The cycling world was ablaze with interest and speculation when the 1968 season began and Merckx did not disappoint anyone.

He began by winning the Tour of Sardinia and followed it up by taking Paris-Roubaix, trouncing the opposition over the infamous 'Hell of the North', and then going on to win the Tour of Romandie.

He was now 22 years old, and pacing himself wisely, had not attempted any of the major stage races up to this point but he entered for the Tour of Italy in 1968 and everyone held their breath to see how this still very young man would fare in such a hard race, second only to the Tour de France in its severity.

Merckx proceeded to wipe the floor with the opposition and the course, notching up four stage wins, overall victory, the King of the Mountains and the Points Classification. There was no department of the race which found him backward. Time trials, flat or hilly, long stages, mountains, sprint finishes, they all came the same to him and he was already being acclaimed as the greatest rider the world had ever known.

He did not ride the Tour de France that year, he was still building up his strength for that milestone in his history but he still scored 27 wins that season. As reigning world champion he was expected to do well in the title race which was being held in Italy on the motor-racing circuit at Imola. He did not, but his faithful lieutenant, Vittorio Adorni, pulled off the most important cycling victory in the world.

Merckx the unselfish, said the papers afterwards, for he was reckoned to have given it to the Italian. Certainly Merckx never attacked when Adorni broke away alone over the last 50 miles and only a Merckx could have caught him that day.

It was a fantastic win by Adorni. Adorni was 31 years old and he won by nearly 9 mins from a big group with Italians taking five of the first six places. They all trooped off with Belgian, Herman Van Springel, who stopped the clean sweep by taking second place, to the anti-doping control.

The unselfishness of Eddy Merckx was much more apparent to me when I watched the finish of the Paris-Tours classic that September. Practically the whole field thundered into the town, sweeping along the main boulevard and, with about 300 metres to the line, Merckx hit the front, going like a train.

It seemed suicidal for a moment until I saw another Faema jersey just behind him. It was his fellow Belgian, Guido Reybrouck and there was the great Merckx leading his team mate out to victory, his way of saying 'thank you' for all the work done during the season.

He ended the Sixties on the highest possible note, winning 43 events including the Tour de France at his first attempt. All his other wins that season, including Milan-San Remo for the third time, were completely overshadowed by his magnificence in that gruelling event, which is in another chapter....

CHAPTER TEN

MARATHON TO NORTH WALES

'The Holyhead'

It is a road steeped in history. The Romans had started it, Watling Street was part of it and Telfer had helped to finish it. The A5, still busy but without its former traffic now that the M1 motorway is in use, runs from Marble Arch to Holyhead.

The road winds its way through fourteen counties of England and Wales, crossing the Menai Bridge to reach the lovely Isle of Anglesey where, along the Newry Beach promenade, it ends at 265 miles.

It was after the West Bromwich to Holyhead and back event in 1959 that the reintroduction of the great race that Percy Stallard master-minded was really thought about. Over a few beers in Holyhead for the overnight stop, Stan Kite and Bobby Thom, amongst others, were telling me about the 1951 race, its excitement and agony, thrills and laughs and it became obvious to me that a legend had been built up about this marathon event, and ever since it took place, there was much speculation as to whether there would ever be another one.

I was working with Corona Soft Drinks at that time and they had just sponsored the West Bromwich event among several other small races that year as part of their publicity programme. It was really seeing these first races and the people who organised and rode them that started me off in cycling.

Completely bitten by the pedal bug I had already begun planning events for Corona's sponsorship in the following year and it seemed almost certain that the Holyhead would be one of them.

Messrs Kite and Thom had spoken so well of the race, their phrases spilling out in disjointed sentences as the memories came flooding back. It sounded terrific and I was sold on the idea right there and then in the bar of the County Hotel, Holyhead.

During my travels the following year I asked many cyclists and ex-riders, too, about the Holyhead and always there was the same enthusiasm, the same feeling of excitement. Although I never saw the first event I was now sharing their sentiments and became anxious to put this dream into reality.

My part in the actual revival of the race was only a small and not very difficult one. Corona had been getting good publicity in the press as well as good crowds at their earlier events and they had no hesitation in approving the Holyhead as one of the events for the 1961 programme.

Having got the money the rest, for me, was easy. Stan Kite, who readily accepted the responsibility of organiser, began to do the real graft, the long hours of meetings, the travelling up the route, the letters to the many Police Forces along the road, finding the officials, sorting out the entries, arranging the programme and all the other things which have to be done.

Backing him were the many and experienced members of the Wolverhampton Wheelers and the hard work and long slog was eventually handed over to the 40 strong field of independents and amateurs on Saturday 27th May, 1961.

The dawn start passed off quietly, the bunch, full of nervous tension, chatted away amiably as they rode out to Edgware to the official start after a long period of neutralisation due to the many sets of traffic lights along the Edgware Road.

There was interest all day with small groups and individuals going off up the road only to be pulled back again. Tricycle record holder, David Duffield, strove valiantly to keep with the race, losing contact four times in all and fighting his way back until that fourth and last time when climbing up to Swallow Falls near Bettws-y-Coed.

It was all happening then and the eventual winner was Albert Hitchen, then riding for Viking Cycles, who took four lengths out of Pete Ryalls, the pair finishing over 2 mins clear of a small group with Viking's George O'Brien gaining third place. Names that have now gone but are certainly not forgotten were in the race.

Famous in their day they were soon to leave the active part of the sport to others. Brian Haskell, Johnnie Pound and Brian Wiltcher were among that group and few of them featured again in the Holyhead which, in 1962, proved 26 mins slower but still more exciting than its predecessor.

Hitchen now wearing a red, white and blue Falcon jersey, was there again but could not pull off his second successive victory due to the close marking by the other two men who shared in the breakaway, the Condor Mackeson riders Denis Tarr and Doug Collins. This was Tarrs' first season as an independent having ridden in the Tour of Britain the previous year as a member of the Combined Services team.

'Diminutive Dennis' won the Skegness-Scarborough stage and, along with Jim Hinds among others, his team earned the nickname of the 'Combine Harvesters', such was their ability to pick up primes and other prizes almost every day.

Despite wearing No. 13 in the race, Tarr was, therefore a force to be reckoned with and one could not forget Collins who, although reaching the end of a fine career, was still a hard man and quite one of the most immaculate stylists in Britain at that time.

The small Londoner, not quite built like Dave Bedwell but about the same height, had a powerful sprint but a broken chain with 60 miles to go and the ensuing chase to rejoin was thought to have tired him too much to offer any great resistance.

His team mate Collins provided more than his share of the pace-making and the two men, naturally fearing Hitchen, tried to rid themselves of this superb Yorkshire rider on the Causeway a few miles before the finish. Everyone should know by now and this is a phrase I have used many times before, 'all is fair in love and war and bike racing' and I feel sure that Hitchen had no resentment for the two London men despite their tactics in trying to drop him.

They failed in their attempt but, on the run in along the Newry Beach Promenade, Hitchen was a beaten man in a

61

tactical sense and, in watching Collins for too long he paid the penalty as Tarr jumped away to take the £100 first prize from him with Collins a close third, all being credited with the same time of 12 hrs 41 mins 55 secs.

Another great race had ended with the crowds improving, the racing standards getting better and the organisation now approaching second to none so that all were eagerly awaiting the event the following year when the big question was, 'Can Hitchen do it again?'

Hitchen was there all right but in the bunch of about 20 riders that contested the sprint which went to a Londoner for the second successive year, Alan Jacob, with that incredible performer Dave Bedwell taking the second place ahead of John Perks (Falcon) and Stan Brittain (Viking Cycles).

It was a close thing with Bedwell, riding for Fred Dean Cycles, nearly pulling off another of his famous sprint victories and little short of amazing when one considers that the 'tiny terror' was winning Tour of Britain stages back in 1951, 12 years prior to the Holyhead event.

An average speed of just over 23 mph for the 265 miles gives an indication as to why there was a bunch finish although those last miles across the Island were always likely to produce a breakaway and there were several men including Bill Bradley, riding for the first time as an independent, prominent but all the efforts came to nothing.

Big John Geddes, riding for Viking, lost what might have been a chance of victory when he broke a crank and crashed, bringing down amateur Pete Ward, just as the bunch turned left on the run-in about 350 yards from the line. Thus Condor-Mackeson gained their second successive win in this now famous classic.

Hitchen's big sprint brought him home yet again in the 1964 race but he had to thank his team mate Bill Holmes who did so much of the work on the long road across the Isle of Anglesey after Hitchen had joined him and Tony Mills (Ryall-Raxar).

They were together just after the third and final feeding

station at Cerrig with nearly 60 miles still to go, only Bill Bradley (Harry Quinn/Everyman Oil) making a big effort to reach them. He chased alone for the rest of the race to finish fourth just over three and a half minutes down having got tantalisingly close, less than a minute, just before the feed and went through that point ignoring the proffered musettes in his vain pursuit.

This was the fastest Holyhead without any doubt, the time of 11 hrs 47 mins 6 secs also including an additional 14 miles where the race left the A5 near Gailey because of road works for the M6 motorway. So 279 miles were covered in that time and despite the distance there were a number of lone breaks including a brave one by amateur Kevin 'Curly' Fairhead, who rode 20 miles alone in an attempt to collect the prime at Chirk for the first rider into Wales.

He failed, his courage out-matching his tactical sense as it often did in road races, but one always remembers him for his aggression in many events, foolhardy though they may have been.

Bernard Burns brought in the bunch, 6¼ mins down to clinch the team victory for the dominant Falcon squad after Doug Collins, now riding in Mills' team, took the fifth place alone nearly 2 mins ahead of them.

One cannot forget the Mottrams Cycles rider, Eddie White who epitomised the courage of a racing cyclist in that Holyhead event of 1964. White, like so many others in the race that year and before, had little chance of victory but, like the classics and the Tour de France, it is an honour to finish.

Eddie finished among the rear group having survived a very nasty crash after about 135 miles. It was just after the race turned back on to the A5 from their detour section near Wolverhampton that it happened.

Unsighted at the rear of the bunch, White rode into a parked motor-cycle at the roadside and seemed out for the count when the St John's Ambulance men, in attendance with the race, ran to him. For a few moments it seemed that his ride had ended as they collected the stretcher from the race Ambulance and

63

set it down alongside his prostrate body on the pavement.

A spare machine had been brought up by one of the service cars and suddenly, quicker than it takes to write it down, White sat up, looked round, made a dash for the spare bike and before anyone could stop him or even speak for that matter, he was off down the road in hot pursuit of the bunch.

The St John's men, cheated of their victim stood there open-mouthed and holding an empty stretcher! Eddie left quite a bit of his skin behind including most of it from his left hand and fingers but, like all men who have set their sights on a particular goal, he bravely continued to Holyhead.

The 1965 event was probably the most famous and the hardest up to that time. It proved, too, to be the end of an era and, as such, is deserving of another chapter. . . .

CHAPTER ELEVEN

HOLYHEAD '65

The Isle of Man apart, professionals had not ridden on the open roads in Britain and it was another ambition of mine to try and make this possible and what better event to choose than the great classic of London to Holyhead?

It was also to be the last time that Corona Soft Drinks would be sponsoring the race, the last time in fact that the company would be involved in cycle racing for some time.

For seven years they had provided financial assistance to many events, along with the Holyhead their most important races in the early Sixties was the Tour of the West and one cannot forget their help with the Merseyside Four Day and the National Schoolboys Championship.

During a seven year period Corona spent at least £35,000 on cycle racing and this splendid contribution to the sport could not be measured in cash alone. I am quite sure that their sponsored events laid the foundations for the growth of the sport in Britain which had been going through a pretty thin time.

The quarrels of the British League of Racing Cyclists and the National Cyclists Union had only recently been resolved by the formation of the British Cycling Federation and it was upon their shoulders, this amalgam of the two rival bodies, that the future of the sport lay. It must have been a most satisfying thing to have such a sponsor in addition to the Milk Marketing Board who were then just beginning to build upon their Tour of Britain.

So Corona were pulling out of cycle racing, using their money for a new side of their expansion programme. It was a pity in a way for they, too, had gained immensely from the publicity and they were losing the most important thing of all in changing their plans, continuity.

An amusing example of this came up later when the Tour of the West found another sponsor. I recall being with their Regional Sales Manager of Truro as the packed streets waited for the race to come through. He asked in a shop what was happening and when told it was the Tour of the West he enquired, subtly, who were the sponsors and the reply came swiftly back, 'Corona'.

Tom Simpson, Shay Elliot, Vin Denson, Barry Hoban and Belgian, René Van Meenen were the riders from abroad who came to tackle this longest single day, unpaced cycle race in the world, pitting their strength and vast experience against the still up and coming independents of Britain. Quite a lot of them had never ridden on the Continent and it was quite possible they were beaten men psychologically long before the 5 a.m. start at Marble Arch.

What a change there was at the point when the riders assembled on the usual date of the last Saturday in May. There must have been about a thousand people there, at least eight hundred more than at previous Holyhead starts! Television film cameras, press men, everything was terrific and the race was soon under way.

Simpson was never far from the front all day and it soon became clear that speed alone would be shaking off quite a number of the 40 strong field long before they reached the Menai Bridge and it proved just so.

There were, naturally enough, many incidents en route, some amusing and others likely to make the blood boil like the attitude of the police in certain areas. I remember seeing one police motor-cyclist waiting behind a telephone box at Dunstable, just beyond a set of lights and obviously there to observe that the letter of the law was obeyed.

Simpson noticed him, too, and he had some hard things to say about traffic and lack of assistance when he got to the finish. It really was absurd and I am only thankful that as the Sixties have reached their later years, police co-operation has improved and, I am sure, will continue to do so.

As the race wound its way into Wales, the Continentals

really made their presence felt and up the climb past Swallow Falls the break seemed complete. It contained all the 'foreign invaders' plus Hitchen, Bill Bradley and Pete Gordon, the 1964 amateur champion now riding for Viking-Trumanns Steel. Hitchen and Bradley were in Falcon colours and the group remained together right to the line.

Simpson tried several times to break away as they rode through the Nant Ffrancon Pass but Hitchen was always alert. It was at this time that the officials began to despair at the ever-increasing numbers of cars that pass, stopped and re-passed the break, obviously sightseers, all cycling enthusiasts who ought to have known better. Some people never learn and never seem to realise that through their own selfish actions they make matters worse for the race as a whole.

Riders can be baulked, others who have broken away can be joined by the rest if a line of cars are strung out behind them and, equally bad, the police can gain a wrong impression at seeing such a hold-up of traffic at the back of a race and regard it as a delay to other road-users.

Some day, and it will happen I am sure, the police will supervise the major events to such an extent that it will be impossible to overtake the riders. It has been done already in some areas, purely because of these fanatical and stupid followers and I know I speak for riders and officials alike when I say 'it can't come soon enough'.

Back to the racing. I think everyone was hoping for a Simpson win although many folk would have been equally happy had the £120 first prize gone to a British-based rider. The eight strong group remained together across the Isle of Anglesey despite there being a number of places ideal of breakaways.

The packed promenade saw a tremendous battle for the line with Simpson getting it by inches from Elliott, who was second, and Hitchen. The Falcon man was the danger to them and Elliott had a hard task to try and control things so that Simpson won.

Foreign professionals who have ridden the Isle of Man and

other events in Britain are renowned for 'ganging up' and sharing out the spoils later. For the British riders to say they are on to a hiding because of it is surely sour grapes for if they liked to form a combine I am certain they could put it across the 'foreigners' by sheer weight of numbers. The biggest problem facing the British riders which is still applicable as I write, is the petty jealousy among themselves which prevents a joint effort for their own good.

There is, of course, no proof that such things occurred but there is always the possibility that the eight men in that winning break could have had a gentleman's agreement and that the prize money would be shared out equally among them afterwards. Who would complain about it? The result was a popular one and the whole group deserved the acclaim they received.

Wherever there is money and top riders in a race one can always twist things around to suit a particular situation. I have brought up this Holyhead finish really as a case in point just to show the sort of unkind and totally unnecessary rumours that follow the finish of a big event.

People are entitled to their own opinions. For my part I am satisfied that justice was done and that if there was to have been a 'fix' it would have occurred long before that big sprint along the Newry Beach Promenade. It is still a matter of conjecture that Elliott 'gave' Simpson the sprint and, if he did, what of it? They were good friends and in cycle racing friends are very essential.

Simpson was his usual talkative self after the presentation, slating the police and oncoming traffic which, he said, 'completely unnerved him at times'. As he rode away waving his bouquet to the cheering crowds who could have foreseen that just twelve weeks later he was to become the world professional road champion?

So the London-Holyhead was at an end after five exciting years but, despite its lapsing from the calendar for the same length of time, I feel it will be back again and there is news as I write that Remington Shavers will be the sponsors in 1970.

CHAPTER TWELVE

'TRIALS AND TRIBULATIONS'

Why does cycling have to be so complicated?

The popularity of cycling sport has ebbed and flowed in Britain ever since the bicycle was invented, the biggest blow and one which is still being felt, was the cancellation of road racing around the turn of the century.

As the road racing men put other users of the public highway in fear and various assortments of horses and carriages to flight it was decided to stop this type of sport. It terminated just about the time that the Tour de France began and, on the Continent, the sport increased steadily.

Not until a small group of men got together and formed the British League of Racing Cyclists in 1942 did road racing come back to Britain and the ensuing struggle for power very nearly finished the sport as far as Britain was concerned.

For about 40 years, while the racing scene abroad grew by leaps and bounds, cycling kept to the straight and narrow paths, the tracks and the time trials with occasional place to place record attempts thrown in for good measure.

The greatest possible credit must be given to Mr F. T. Bidlake for devising the time trial as a means of keeping the sport alive and, at the same time, preventing any further displeasure from the police and public on the roads.

There has been little change basically in this typically English section of cycling since the North Road Cycling Club ran a 50 mile time trial in October 1895 and there are few alterations today apart from the machines themselves.

Time trialing continued steadily, the faithful few enlarging to promote many events and the sport grew until 1922 when the Road Racing Council was formed as a body to link organisers but there were no special rules or even a system.

Other than track racing it was the only sport open to racing enthusiasts and, although items on cycling in the newspapers were few and far between, its growth eventually demanded national control and in 1937 the Road Time Trials Council was born.

They provided rules, agreed on set courses for various distances and generally gave cycling a shot in the arm. There was not much in the way of publicity though for one of their rules was that all events should be private and confidential until the results were known and, in any case, the early morning starts in country lanes proved something of a deterrent to those who knew and wanted to attend.

There was good reason for this cloak of secrecy, brought about partly by cautiousness and through remembering those early days when cycling on the roads got itself into trouble. By keeping the events closed from the general news there would be no vast crowds to disrupt the Sunday morning highways and byways and the Council even devised a very clever scheme to assist in all their plans.

This was to give all the approved and carefully measured courses a code number with weekend numbers also, the opening week of the season being 'Week 1' and so on and only those within the sport itself really knew when and where a particular event was going to take place.

After the war cycling had the League to further its cause for publicity and they did a tremendous job but not without meeting some opposition, mainly from the National Cyclists' Union, then governing body of the track sport. Arguments raged up and down the country and, despite riders and officials being banned for life by the Union, the League continued to thrive and even made a number of breakthroughs in British cycling sport.

Without doubt their greatest achievement was in organising the first Tour of Britain, sponsored by the *Daily Express*, and this really put cycling on the map. Petty jealousies, disbeliefs, arguments and even hatred abounded, the squabbles eventually terminating in the formation of the British Cycling Federation in 1959.

The troubles caused by petty officialdom and the open dislike for each other by the warring bodies threw cycling into chaos and the *Daily Express* looked elsewhere for some of their publicity activities after 1954.

The newly formed Federation, containing men from both the former competing groups, disgruntledly got down to sorting out cycling's problems, problems which the Road Time Trials Council were not really concerned about but they, too, had to consider the change in the sport and the attitudes of the enthusiasts and public.

They were slow to act and the 'no publicity rule' was only waived in 1962 at their Annual Meeting by which time the Federation had got on its feet and road racing had grown in popularity and numbers by leaps and bounds.

The Tour of Britain was back in the calendar thanks to the Milk Marketing Board. There were a number of other good sponsors and the future was beginning to brighten. The antipathy of the League and the Union slowly but surely died away, flaring up occasionally through the short-sightedness of a few fanatics but there were new undertones now.

The Federation and the Council should amalgamate so that one body controlled all cycle sport was the whispering campaign that grew louder as the months passed. Road racing man or time trialist – which was the better rider? Arguments began again and all the same silly jealousies were afire once more.

Joint rules were eventually formulated between the two bodies despite the Federation putting forward a motion at one Annual Meeting to break away from the RTTC and the battles rage on, fortunately by word alone.

Is there a case for both sides? The Federation governs all road and track racing and are the only officially recognised body internationally. They employ a full-time paid General Secretary and a National Coach. They finance riders and teams to go abroad to represent Great Britain and, despite mistakes since they were formed, have done an excellent job in the past 12 years.

The Road Time Trials Council are not recognised internationally – they concern themselves only with time trials in England and Wales. Like the Federation they get a Government grant annually but all their officials hold honorary positions.

The Council have made a splendid contribution to British cycling over the years and are still doing so, providing a high standard of organisation with all their top events and giving an opportunity both to young and old alike to enjoy their chosen sport.

Let them remain introspective and concern themselves with their own affairs but, is this possible? The RTTC want to share in road racing, imposing their authority on time trials run in big stage races like the Tour of Britain. This is not their fault for it is all in the Joint Agreement with the Federation so is it the Federation who are to blame?

No, it is neither body. It is a ridiculous situation that exists because so many Federation officials have been brought up on time trials and there are too many old men, set in their ways, who stick at the top of various levels of the sport.

Decisions are shelved far too often and it has been said that if you were to remove the trousers of all the big-wigs of cycling you would find a large red mark across the crotch where they have sat on the fence for years.

Money is involved of course with the Council rich and the Federation poor for fairly obvious reasons. Jealousy is there, too, the Federation gaining the glamour and the publicity, the RTTC having nothing but the satisfaction of a job well done and many years standing behind them.

Pride comes into it, too, and yet the simple answer is amalgamation for cycling as a whole would benefit. The two controlling bodies have made people regard time trialing and road racing as two separate sports when, in fact, they are a combination of one, both requiring great skill and stamina.

So much nonsense has been talked about the merits of one

part of the sport against the other that it is a waste of paper to bother to enlarge upon it. Sufficient to say that the two are essential and it has been a long-standing mistake by the British enthusiast to treat the time trial and the road race as opposites. Comparisons cannot be made for they go together like bread and cheese and no one would try to compare one of those two commodities with the other.

One excellent example of the combination is the great Frenchman, Jacques Anquetil who won the Tour de France five times. Time trials helped him to victory but he could never have achieved success if he had not been a road man, too.

I am afraid that indoctrination over the years for one side of the sport or the other, will prevent many people reading this from taking another viewpoint.

If they are so old-fashioned and set in their ways as to not see that amalgamation can bring better cycling with so many benefits for all, including greater international success, then the sport in Britain is doomed to the limbo it rests in at the moment, for many years to come.

CHAPTER THIRTEEN

'SIMPSON'

On the thirteenth day of July, on the thirteenth stage of the Tour de France, Tom Simpson, whose race number was 49, which added together makes thirteen, collapsed and died on Mont Ventoux, a victim of heat exhaustion and altitude.

Looking at the 'thirteens' it was a great day for the superstitious but it was a tragic and terrible loss to countless thousands both at home and abroad. Simpson was British cycling and the saddest thing of all was that he died under a cloud with that awful word 'dope' uppermost in most ordinary people's minds.

The facts cannot be denied. He had taken an amphetamine-based drug, an artificial stimulant. It was all there in the report after his body had been examined but what was never said was whether he died as a result of it. The autopsy stated only that he died through the intense heat and lack of oxygen but the stigma will remain.

I think the drug played a very small part in his death. I think it relieved him of much of the pain and suffering as he fought to retain his place on that mountainous stage in the burning heat.

He was a close friend of mine and naturally I would want to defend him and his name and, knowing him as I did, I am quite convinced that Tom Simpson killed himself because he just did not know when to stop. All his racing life he had punished his frail body, pushing it to the limits of endurance with his tremendous will-power and single-mindedness and, on Mont Ventoux, he pushed it too far, perhaps the drug easing the pain of it all.

I cannot defend him for taking drugs. He was wrong but he was not alone for the whole system was wrong with far too many riders doing exactly the same thing with the authorities turning a blind eye to it all. Under pressures from sponsors, with big money at stake, with reputations to make or maintain, watched by millions and, most important of all, with the event becoming harder and more spectacular each year, the men who rode this fiendish race, for that's what it had become, sought for a less painful way of taking their punishment.

You could give a cart-horse drugs but it would not win the Derby and the same applies in cycling. You have to be a very good rider at the outset before drugs really assist. Simpson was a very good rider but so were the members of the group that were ahead of him on the road and there is little doubt that they, too, had indulged in this awful practice.

Simpson took drugs that day not to win but to stay with the leaders because he knew he could not match them. Because he knew that drug-taking was rife on the Tour and he was not going to be beaten by a pill.

He was defeated though, but by a set of circumstances which combined to beat his body but not his mind. Even at the moment of death as he collapsed he was still willing his tortured frame up that climb. His fingers had to be prised from the 'bars and his teeth, gritted together, had to be similarly dealt with before the 'kiss of life' could be administered. It was too late.

By his death Simpson, who had helped British cycling throughout his life, made his final contribution to the sport he loved. Just as his fellow countrymen had done their share two years before with their own particular brand of courage (see Chapter 17) Simpson now opened the eyes of the world to the evils of drug taking in the sport.

The results are there for all to see. Anti-doping controls at the world championships, the classics, the Tour de France and many other events, too, have helped to rid cycling of this terrible scourge. It has not disappeared completely yet but things are well on the way.

Another pointer is the number of new men who have come to the fore in professionalism after a dope-free career as amateurs. Even more pronounced has been the almost total eclipse of many famous names, unable to win because the opportunities to cheat are so few.

Many people, while agreeing with the tests and changes, have asked why it had to be Simpson that fate chose to provide this eye-opener to the world, this necessary reminder to the administrators in sport. Why could it not have been a lesser-known man, whose loss to cycling would never have been felt with such magnitude?

The answer is quite simple. It *had* to be a Simpson, a great rider, otherwise the publicity and the obvious need for reform would never have transpired. So in thanking Tom Simpson for what he did during his life we must also remember him for the after-effects of his supreme sacrifice.

For myself I shall remember him in so many different ways, as a great rider, as an amusing companion, a family man and, above all, a 'character'. He was a remarkable man whose quiet and normal up-bringing was never really changed by the success he achieved. I have heard him talking to young riders, his own associates, Prime Ministers and other dignitaries with the same openness and frankness, his audience on each occasion, attentive and relaxed.

People in Britain could not realise just what he meant to the Continent, particularly the Belgians who regarded him as one of their own. The greatest injustice was done to him by the popular press in this country, only really reporting his major successes in large type.

I wrote in a final chapter in the second edition of his book *Cycling is my life* which I helped him to produce, 'the British press had a field day when he died'. Of all the magnificent rides, victories and achievements that Simpson had it was ironic that his biggest coverage came when he could not longer read it.

The laws of libel and slander prevent me from printing his views on the attitude of the British press to cycling in general. As forthright and as outspoken as usual he felt that their lack of coverage on a sport that featured as 'number one' on the Continent, was unbelievable and it was possibly the major reason for its lack of growth in Britain.

I have heard the crowds all over Europe chanting, 'Seem-son, Seem-son!' and his popularity had to be seen to be believed. It was probably in the Six Day events that he was so dearly loved because of his clowning as well as his excellent riding.

Simpson gave the public what they wanted and the more they laughed the more he would provide the entertainment. To see him clown his way through a 'Devil', known as an 'Elimination' on the Continent, was a delight. He would have the crowd on its feet in excitement at one moment and then roaring with laughter the next as he hung off the tail of the field and then suddenly sprinted into a gap leaving someone else with his back wheel over the line.

I saw him in Milan doing just this but also carrying a whistle which he would blow, pointing at the unfortunate rider he had just eliminated, at the same time. In Ghent once he clowned his way right through to the final where he met the Italian Giuseppe Beghetto, the then reigning world sprint champion.

The Sportspaleis was humming with excitement as the pair set out for the final sprint. They desperately wanted Simpson to win but knew he stood no chance, as Tom himself knew, too. Even with no chance he still had the crowd on its feet and screaming with laughter. Tom went for a long one off the banking with a lap to go and Beghetto, playing it cleverly for the crowd, did not get alongside until the final banking. By then Simpson was 'cooked' but in a superb display of bike handling and clowning as Beghetto went past him, he leaned forward over the 'bars and with one arm extended, pretended to hold the Italian's seat pillar.

How does one end a story about Tom Simpson? Perhaps the best way is to repeat a story he loved to tell and one which rocked the audience at the Sports Writers' Dinner when he was guest of honour as 'Sportsman of the Year' in 1965.

Strangely enough it was about doping but in horse racing

and Simpson delighted his listeners, including Prime Minister Harold Wilson, with this anecdote.

At a race meeting the Chief Steward, the Duke of Norfolk, saw a trainer giving a horse something in the paddock before the start. When he asked what it was, the trainer pulled some lumps of sugar from his pocket and replied, 'Just a few lumps of sugar, Your Grace. The horse likes it and it gives you energy, I like some as well, now and again.' And he ate a few lumps, proffering some to the Duke who accepted them and went off chewing and crunching the sugar.

The trainer saw his jockey mounted and then gave him his last minute instructions. 'Now,' he said, 'Don't forget, hold him back for the first few furlongs and then give him his head – and if anyone passes you don't get worried, it'll either be me or the Duke of Norfolk!'

CHAPTER FOURTEEN

'WEST COUNTRY STYLE'

There are several good clubs down around Bristol, Somerset and Devon, all of them having produced good riders in the past and containing, every year, excellent material for the future. Unfortunately the West Country seems to be out on a limb, and far from the selectors' eyes.

If some of their top men had been given an international opportunity earlier there might have been a few more medals for Britain. I am thinking in particular of Brian Sandy, for many years the pride of Taunton. Sandy's biggest problem in his early years was perhaps his inability to concentrate on one aspect of the sport. He rode in everything, time trials, road races, track events on tarmac and grass and, although he gained a national title in the latter, I feel he was best suited as a roadman-sprinter.

Sandy in a bunch finish was a master and yet he did not really gain proper recognition until he was 30 years of age, being then chosen for the British track team in the Tokyo Olympics. By that time he had probably reached or even passed his best as a track man.

There were a number of others, with the Mid-Devon Road Club producing Roy Hopkins and the same club having twice professional road champion, Colin Lewis, still one of the hardest and shrewdest men in the business. Derek Green from Bristol was another man whose potential was never properly tapped but, towards the end of the Sixties several men out West have been noticed.

Young Phil Edwards, former junior champion on the road is one and another is Gary Crewe, both of them hailing from Bristol, having learnt their racing on some hard circuits round the Mendips.

If the West had some good racing men they were also blessed with good organisers, some of them coming from the same small club. This is the Bath Olympic Cycling Club, no longer producing men for competition but supplying the brains for numerous events.

Bill Rains, former Treasurer of the 'League' was at its head and it was this outwardly calm and shrewd Bristolian who requires grateful thanks from cycling for his efforts in putting on so many top races in the area during the Sixties.

It was Rains who first assisted in building up the Tour of the South West from a one day race in 1959 and 1960 to the big eight day professional race that took place in 1968. It was really the sponsorship of Corona Soft Drinks that began it all and through their financial help another cycling milestone was passed.

Cycling went 'West' quite literally when the Tour of the South West raced into Cornwall in 1963 for the first time. In the previous year the race had reached four day proportions, starting at Weston Super Mare and going across Exmoor to the North Devon resort of Ilfracombe. It then swung across Devon and into Paignton and took in the last day going back up to Weston where there was usually a race round the Mendips to sort things out.

It was still a good race back in 1962 even over just the four days and I can recall some of the excitement and amusement of that event which was won by Albert Hitchen of Falcon Cycles.

A youngster from Manchester caught everyone's eye both by his aggressive and courageous riding and his peculiar style. His name was Peter Gordon who, two years later, was to take the British amateur road title. Gordon has featured many times in top events in Britain since that occasion and his style, if it can be called that, has earned him many nicknames. 'Twitch', 'Noddy', 'Flash', 'The Hairpin' are some of them, mainly because of his thin frame but, believe me, what Gordon may have lacked in brawn and muscle he made up for in sheer teeth-gritting, never-give-up guts. Many riders, better equipped physically, were unable to thrash their bodies to a state of exhaustion as Gordon did so frequently. If they could have possessed such determination then a world title could have been theirs.

The amusement on that race was not Gordon but his father, Alf. Visiting the area for the first time, Alf Gordon was carried away by the organisation and the racing itself. On the third stage from Ilfracombe his son was in the break with Hitchen and several others and Alf's car was becoming a nuisance and a problem and it was stopped eventually by Rains at the roadside.

It was not an official car and, therefore, should not have been following, particularly as young Gordon was in the race. A white-faced Alf Gordon stepped out and, before Bill Rains could say a word, Alf spoke. 'I know I'm doing wrong,' he said, 'but I just can't stop myself because this is such a cracking race.' The problem was soon sorted out and the two men became firm friends.

To get back to the race that year, young Gordon took second overall place, 25 secs behind winner Hitchen. The fresh-faced Sheffield lad who won the last stage into Weston went on to take the Commonwealth Games gold medal that year. Wes Mason was his name and we were to hear a lot about that dry character with the wry smile in the years to come.

The memory for me on that race was a superb chase on the third stage by Hugh Porter and Gil Taylor. Both riding for the Midlands they produced a terrific two-up team time trial which was a joy to watch. At times they were like a tandem in action, their long legs thrusting the pedals round in complete unison.

In 1963 the event covered six days and had the Cornish folk out at the roadside clapping and cheering as if they had seen bike racing all their lives. Hitchen won it again but it was a close battle and everyone enjoyed the event which also contained many incidents.

One was at the finish at Penzance where the field came through the dock area and then along the seafront. A large

F

81

coal lorry decided to try and beat the bunch to the line, the vocal efforts of the race officials, police and crowd having no effect at all on the apparently deaf driver. He lumbered along, the mass of charging riders closing all the time and the lorry got the sprint by about a wheel! The Mayor remarking afterwards that he was never going to buy his coal from there again!

The following year, with more money for the organisation, the race improved again. Bill Holmes, now riding for Falcon Cycles, led throughout with well-known names taking some stages. Dave Bedwell won into Penzance, Chisman took the long one from Penzance to Paignton and fog stopped the race on Bodmin Moor.

This was on the stage from Ilfracombe to Newquay. Across the lonely Moor in cold and fog, which reduced visibility to about 30 yards, the bunch came down like a pack of cards when someone's brake cable snapped. No one was badly hurt but the incident caused the Chief Commissaire, Roy Thame, to stop the race. Wisely it was neutralised on the steep descent into Bodmin. (Pete Gordon was happy with the decision as he was off the back at the time!)

One of the officials, Stan Crick, then produced a phrase which will long be remembered in the West Country. Organiser Rains was waiting just outside Bodmin when Crick arrived, post haste, and screamed across the road to him, 'There's been a cock-up in the fog on Bodmin!' The general amusement afterwards as Bill Rains explained it was that Stan was standing right outside the County Mental Hospital at the time and everyone thought he was trying to gain admittance!

It was to be the last Corona sponsored event in 1965 and the race took in eight days that year with Bill Bradley emerging overall winner as a member of the Falcon team who again dominated the event. It was still open to amateurs and independents and a French team added a little atmosphere but failed to get much out of it in the way of prizes.

Still covering eight days the event took place again in 1966 under the sponsorship of Senior Service and it was Chisman's

turn to take overall victory. It was his strong riding that year
that brought forth the comment from Bill Holmes at Newquay
at the end of a stage, 'There he goes. Off to get his bucket of
water and a bale of hay for his tea!'

This comment earned 'Chis', always a great work-horse, the
endearing nickname of 'Arkle', one which stuck with him
throughout the rest of his racing years.

There was no race in 1967, Senior Service having pulled out
of all sponsorship, including horse-racing that year and it was
to be another tobacco firm that took up the running in 1968,
when the best-ever Tour took place. Sponsored by Player's
No. 6, the eight day event contained three teams from the
Continent and the now fully professional teams in Great
Britain.

There were a number of short circuit evening races in the
itinerary, all of them being won by a small Dutchman, Harm
Ottenbros of Willem II-Gazelle. Ottenbros went on to win the
world title in Zolder in 1969 but the Tour was won, quite
splendidly, by Arthur Metcalfe, riding for Carlton Cycles.

Petty jealousies in British cycling nearly ruined the race
before it began. Rumours about the prize list and the total
contribution the sponsors were making got completely out of
hand. It was all supposition but it worked like yeast, fermenting
various elements until the riders in Britain were ready to try
and boycott the race.

The main target in all this farce seemed to be Bill Rains
mainly because he had been very successful but also, I feel,
because there were rumours that he was being paid for running the event. I cannot see why he should not have been since
good organisers are hard to find and if a few more were paid
for their services cycle races might be organised a bit better.

Whatever the case Rains was very much on his own and he
threw all the problems out of the window by making the event
an invitation only affair, asking the major British teams to
enter and providing travelling expenses for them.

Outwardly Rains remained calm but I am sure he was very
upset and must have felt much the same as I had done after

the New Brighton affair. (See Chapter 22.) The professionals were behaving in a similar manner and endangering their own future and livelihood but, thanks to the prompt action by Rains, the disaster of New Brighton never repeated itself.

The silly thing was that arrangements had been made for travelling expenses for riders but, inflamed by a few misguided individuals who were stirring up the old argument about foreign riders getting a better deal, the whole affair got completely out of hand.

I am sure the majority had no idea of what was involved in organising a big Tour. Certainly they could have had little notion of what the expense, to say nothing of the work, totalled. Right from the selected route and police approval down to providing vehicles, petrol, accommodation for officials, printing programmes, hiring loudspeaker equipment, purchasing riders' numbers, pins, flags, routing arrows, the cost of postages and telephone calls all coming out of the budget with a host of other necessary items.

When the Tour was under way it never failed to be a delight to travel with it. Everything that should have been there was in its place even down to prime flags which were, themselves, a reflection on the organisation. I cannot ever recall seeing flags in better condition than down in the West Country.

I know it is only a small thing but the number of times I have seen mother's blue towel draped on a hedge to mark the start of a prime or a torn piece of black and white check tablecloth for the finish line, make one thankful of the good organisers.

Of course Bill Rains was not just an organiser he was a cycling man through and through, devoting much of his time to officiate at various events in the West as well as arranging other races and giving advice when needed.

His home had an ever open door to bike riders and officials who would invade the neat semi-detached villa just outside the city many times during a season. The bottles of excellent home made wine would be brought out from under the stairs, camp beds and extra mattresses and blankets would be dragged from cupboards and the family table stretched to its limits.

That table, I am sure, was only designed for eight people at the most and yet at times, it must have had at least fourteen people sardined around it with several others in armchairs, eating from trays. Afterwards would come the endless chat about riders, races, rules and stories, some true, some clean and many dirty.

This was a typical cycling house, the kindness and hospitality only exceeded by the company itself. There are many homes like this all over the country where I have been happy to stay on numerous occasions as, I am sure, have many who read this book.

The 1968 Tour of the West was a great success and it came as a big surprise when Player's backed down the following year. Whatever their reasons were for discontinuing their very fine financial help I only hope it had nothing to do with the troubles that arose before the event began in 1968. Rumours, however unfounded they may be, are hard to disprove and the damage done by a handful of misguided folk is difficult to assess.

I suppose back-biting and petty jealousy is part of life generally whether in sport or business but the harm it does is impossible to measure.

During the latter part of the Sixties the Bath Olympic Club have been active in organising an event for W. D. & H. O. Wills. This has steadily improved from its small beginnings, much as the Corona Tour did, and it reached the stature of a three-day event in 1969.

It would be no surprise to me to see it blossom forth into another really big professional Tour and one naturally expects that Bill Rains, despite having been forced into an early retirement because of a bad heart in 1969, will grace the scene with his well-known calm, cigar-smoking figure.

CHAPTER FIFTEEN

THE MUD-PLUGGERS

After 20 years of world Cyclo-Cross Championships it is really nothing short of amazing that those titles have been shared only among five men apart from Jean Robic of France who took the first world title event in 1950. His fellow countryman Roger Rondeaux then won the next three to be followed by another Frenchman, Andre Dufraisse, who won for the five succeeding years.

Then it was Italy's turn with the great Renato Longo winning the first of his five titles, separated by West German Rolf Wolfshohl in 1960, 1961 and again in 1962. Longo interrupted a hat trick of wins for Belgian Erik De Vlaeminck to take his fifth title in Zurich in 1967.

Such domination is quite remarkable and, for three of them, they have hardly ever been out of the top placings when they didn't win. Dufraisse also has two silver and four bronze medals; Wolfshohl is the other way round, four silver and two bronze while Longo took two silvers and a bronze.

That is Cyclo-Cross, always seeming to be dominated by just a handful of men, the rest just also-rans and it has been much the same in Britain where 'Cross began rather later than on the Continent as one would expect of our slow-cycling nation.

Cyclo-Cross had its 'Criterium International' before world championships were instituted in 1950, and the very one was run back in 1924. There had been some attempts to run events in Britain and although the famous Bagshot Scramble was being staged before the Second World War, nothing was properly organised until the British Cyclo-Cross Association was formed in 1960.

Before that time though, quite a number of people had been

bitten by the mud bug and the first National Championship was run at Welwyn in 1955. It was won by that great all-round rider Alan Jackson of the De Laune Cycling Club who took it again the following year at Halesowen, the same year that he took the bronze medal in the Olympic Road Race in Melbourne.

For the next two years it was the turn of Don Stone, from the 34th Nomads Cycling Club and he was followed by Barry Spence, Wolverhampton Wheelers and in 1960 it was Dave Briggs, Saracen Road Club.

Then, in 1961, came a name that was to stay at the top for a number of years, John Atkins of the Coventry Road Club. Atkins won in 1962 as well and then came a period of illness which put him out of the running. So, from 1963 until 1965, someone else stepped in to provide the domination, Mick Stallard, son of the famous Wolverhampton man who helped found the British League of Racing Cyclists and Organiser of the first London-Holyhead race.

Stallard took three titles in a row and then bowed out gracefully as Atkins made his come-back in 1966. The small, fair-haired Coventry man made mincemeat of anyone and everyone, always winning with ease for the next two years.

By then there were professionals in Britain and, while in events all over the world, pros and amateurs raced against each other, the situation changed for world and national title events, each being run for separate categories.

Thus, in 1969, Atkins contested the British professional title and won again, still without finding anyone to really test him. The amateur championship, both events being held at Coventry in Allesley Park, was expected to be won by Roger Page, almost the eternal second of British 'Cross, having been beaten so many times in previous seasons by either Atkins or Stallard.

Incredibly though, 'Big Roger' could not make it, for he was passed within the last two miles by his own team mate, Barry Moss of the Solihull Cycling Club. So Roger was second again but what a tremendously courageous rider he was. He never gave up and provided a shining example to the youngsters who were, by 1965, beginning to enjoy the mudlarks.

Interest for schoolboys had grown so much that the Association ran the first Championship for them in 1964 and, while the entry was reasonable in terms of numbers, there was a lot to be desired in their approach and equipment. I recall seeing a lot of non-racing machines, football shorts and plimsolls knocking around but, the spirit was there, and this was the important thing.

The Schoolboy Championship of 1969 was quite a different kettle of fish with getting on for 200 entries and all of them with gleaming racing bikes, proper shorts, all the gear in fact, which must have set their parents back quite a bit!

Cyclo-Cross was a bit of a joke in the early Sixties, a number of the competitors riding for a bit of fun after spending lunchtime in a pub near the course. Some of them still do but there is a far greater awareness and keenness nowadays which suggests that the winter sport of cycling can only improve.

With so many up and coming schoolboys and juniors the future looks bright although a little more money poured into the sport would help a lot. *The Daily Telegraph*, by its sponsorship of the British Championships since 1965 has done a great deal in putting Cyclo-Cross on the map and in its splendid presentation of the events through the hard work of the association and its officials.

One cannot leave the British Cyclo-Cross scene without talking about another man who has constantly been in the headlines but put out of the chance of a national title for a number of years by Atkins and Stallard. I refer to that very likeable Londoner, Keith Mernickle, who took the professional title in the 1966–67 season.

Here was a natural 'Cross man if ever I saw one but the gay life and the enjoyment of parties seemingly took its toll of Mernickle's strength. He was never hard enough on himself and although he trained regularly, like so many other mudpluggers, he would end the day with a foaming pint in his hand.

That has been the problem with the sport, no one would

take it seriously but now, with more money, better organisation, an ever-increasing junior class and higher standards of competition, the pints are being lowered less over a weekend of racing. Temptation is there of course because it's winter time and the social season of cycling is in full swing with dozens of club 'Annual Dinners'. Get thee behind me, Satan!

On the world scene the British riders have not had much success, for a long time Mernickle's great ride in the 1963 world title race at Overboelare in Belgium when he finished 11th in a top field of mainly full professionals, was the best we could claim.

For much of the race he shared the lead with Longo and several other stars but the speed and distance told on him over the last few miles and he dropped back. Even so he got his photograph in the Belgian papers the next day and received considerable acclaim for his ride.

Atkins was the next man to raise our hopes and his chance came in Luxembourg in 1968 when Britain probably fielded their strongest ever team. It was the last time Atkins was to ride as an amateur, the world championships being split by this time, and with Roger Page also in the squad, there were high hopes.

It was a dry but bitterly cold February day with a tough course but most of the muddy sections being frozen and rutted. There was a good section of road with a slight uphill rise to the finish with the usual total distance of about 14 miles to cover.

As the last lap began it was still anybody's race from the dozen or so men at the front. Atkins and Page were there as they crossed the finish line for the final time, 'Big Roger' holding seventh position with Atkins about 12th.

From my vantage point on the road near the packed stands I could see quite a bit of the course and as they came belting along a canal towpath with about three-quarters of a mile to go, my heart was in my mouth.

Page was still hammering away in seventh spot with Atkins beginning to make ground as Roger De Vlaeminck of Belgium attacked at the front. They sped over the rutted path and under the bridge to begin the final climb up towards the road which left them just 400 yards to the line. Somewhere, lost to my view, Page suffered the most awful luck before he reached the road. As Atkins was still forging ahead and making up ground, Page punctured, right there with the last dash for the line almost at hand.

I watched them coming up the road towards the line, desperately looking for a Great Britain jersey. Suddenly, there it was, crossing the line in fifth place, but it was Atkins and I could not for a minute understand what had happened to Roger until I saw him, flat tyre and all, finishing in 14th place, crying with rage and disappointment. He dismounted as he crossed the line and threw his machine up the road, anywhere out of his sight would do!

We can only talk about the 'ifs and buts' now and that finish in Luxembourg will still burn the midnight oil for a long time to come. Britain came pretty close to a Cyclo-Cross medal that cold Sunday afternoon, 'ifs and buts' excluded, and it cannot be very much longer before we see that blue jersey with the red sleeves up on the victory rostrum.

Incidentally, history was made that day. Young Roger De Vlaeminck stayed ahead to win and later in the afternoon his elder brother, Erik took the professional title for the second time in his career.

De Vlaeminck first won the title at Beasain in Northern Spain in 1966 when Longo had punctured in the first few laps right between the two service areas and had no chance of fighting back.

The tall, lean Italian seemed to make a habit of taking revenge for he beat the Belgian out of sight the following year in Zurich on an absolute sea of mud, which, combined with a very hard course, had everyone struggling.

One of the secrets of Longo's success that day was changing to a clean machine on every lap. The Italian helpers quickly washed away the clinging mud which stuck in the forks, chain, spokes and everywhere possible, handing over a light and ready-to-ride bike each time their champion came through the pits.

For myself I found Longo to be the best of all the muddied performers. Always a complete professional he never failed to put on a marvellous display, even when he was beaten. This attitude of the Italian was never more obvious than in his own country at Cavaria, not far from Milan, in the world title race in 1965.

He had won the previous year after Rolf Wolfshohl had the measure of him in Calais in 1962 but it was rumoured that the West German was out to turn the tables on the bronzed, handsome Italian who, many were saying was finished at the age of 28.

Nothing was further than the truth as it happened but what a tremendous battle took place between those two men. A good course, a fine day and an enormous crowd provided a wonderful setting for one of the closest world title races on record.

For lap after lap they matched each other, leaving the rest of the field floundering in the mud behind them. On the running sections where small hurdles and ditches had been craftily arranged, they were stride for stride and it seemed that they were inseparable.

Wolfshohl had started fast, opening up a gap of nearly half a minute on the first lap but Longo had fought his way up to him within a lap, pushing and riding his way through the jostling bunch which threatened to hamper his efforts.

Now, as they began the final lap it was, perhaps, the crowd who took a hand in things. Getting on for 50,000 were packed round the circuit and as the leading pair began the last, killing circuit, a great roar of 'Longo, Longo', went up to the grey skies full of snow which had thankfully refrained from falling.

The reaction from Longo was understandable. He put on the pressure at every turn and twist of the course. From my position in the Grandstand there was a superb view of most of the route which ran parallel with the finishing straight over the last quarter mile and it was here that Longo began to pull ahead.

Almost imperceptibly at first the Italian gained ground. As the pair reached the stretch of hurdles for the last time he was about two lengths clear of Wolfshohl, both men gulping in air madly, their legs moving machine-like in the final phase of this torturing ride. The crowd were screaming now and with an almost deafening crescendo the Italian pulled away. Wolfshohl had nothing left to counter attack and, for the last time, Longo slung the machine from his shoulder on to the tarmac, leapt into the saddle and rode away for his fourth gold medal.

Sheer pandemonium followed his crossing the line a handful of seconds ahead of the plucky West German. The police moved along the route but eventually proved helpless and hopeless in preventing what took place. A great mass of spectators behind a high, wirenetting fence, just to my left and beyond the finish line, suddenly went berserk with delight at their hero.

They smashed down the fence and ran, a great charging garlic-smelling mass of humanity. They immediately over-ran the stands which began to creak and groan with the additional unanticipated weight. Television sets, in various places, provided for the Press and guests to see parts of the course not visible to them, were knocked over and smashed as the fans rampaged through to reach the podium.

I clutched my notes and pen, moving to the back out of the way of the seething mass and watched the struggle, glad to be out of the 'line of fire'. The crush was so large that one could imagine ribs cracking under the strain as the packed finish area swayed to and fro while the police ineffectually fought to provide a path for the later finishers.

Suddenly I saw a Great Britain jersey. It was Coventry's Mick Ives who appeared to be in danger of having his bike wrapped round him as he desperately tried to force a way through to reach the changing rooms. He was obviously worn out after the ride and had little strength left so I vacated my comfortable position and attempted to reach him.

It took me about 5 mins to travel the 20 yards or so to get alongside him. Manners were not applicable any more for it would have been quite useless to have said 'Excuse me,' and waited for someone to step politely aside! It seemed a good opportunity for me to get out, too, and make my way to the Press Room and so I grabbed a rather surprised Ives and began shouting at the top of my voice some of the very few Italian words I knew.

Yelling, 'Attenzione, prago!' and various British pleasantries suitable to the occasion and holding on to Ives, both of us using the bike as a battering ram, we made our way through the milling throng and into breathable and less suffocating surroundings.

Like life, Cyclo-Cross is full of surprises!

CHAPTER SIXTEEN

MERCKX'S TOUR DE FRANCE

With only seven days of the 1969 Tour of Italy left, the then race leader, Eddy Merckx, was disqualified for having allegedly taken artificial stimulants. To say that the cycling world was shocked when the announcement came is an understatement, for everything was in turmoil.

Merckx had won three stages of the race took the lead on stage 9, lost it again three days later and regained it on stage 14 only to be thrown out after the following day's run. Merckx protested his innocence to no avail and his Faema team pulled out in sympathy after all of them had voluntarily given a sample.

There must be some criticism of the way in which the situation was handled by the Italians in charge of the anti-doping controls. A problem arose over the sample Merckx gave which was eventually said to contain an amphetamine-based drug. After a sample is taken it is split into two bottles, one being sent for analysis while the other is kept for a second check if the first proves positive.

It is a formal rule to protect the rider who can then have the sample independently analysed but, in any case, the rider should be told immediately the first sample is found to be positive. Merckx was not told before they proceeded with the second sample. Italy came in for some sharp comment over the laxity of these controls and it was quite obvious, reading between the lines, that the Italians were thought to have 'framed' Merckx. Jealous about their own big race they could well have got fed up with Merckx beating Gimondi in Belgium and France but, in their own country they found a way to stop him.

In the ensuing hue and cry Merckx went into hiding saying that unless he was proved innocent he would not ride the Tour de France. For the riders in the Tour of Italy, the bottom fell out of the race and Gimondi, second overall at the time of the Belgian's disqualification, refused to wear the 'Maglia Rosa' at the start of the stage. Donning his national road champion's jersey, he was quoted as saying, 'Even if I win the Giro, it has no significance as Merckx is no longer in the race.'

The matter was investigated by the FICP, the professional body affiliated to the UCI, and they met in Belgium to consider the appeal by Merckx with less than a fortnight to go before the Tour de France began. Eight men deliberated for over four hours before returning a 'not guilty' verdict. Merckx was cleared!

Along with the organisers of the French Tour and countless millions of fans, Merckx breathed a sigh of relief and set about training again quickly for he had not touched his bike for at least ten days. There was quite an uproar from riders as a result of the decision, many of them having been suspended in the past for taking artificial stimulants. One law for the rich and another for the poor was the general cry from the men who had been tested in the same way but had always had any appeal turned down.

The arguments will rage for many years to come but Merckx shut his mind to everything, concentrating only on his aim to win the Tour de France at his first attempt, and training time was running out for him. Twelve days to go and he was madly riding 200 kilometres a day behind motors and managed to race in just four criterium events and one road race over 200 kilometres, the Belgian Championship, which he did not win, before time ran out.

The Tour de France, the greatest sporting test of human endurance, began in Roubaix, scene of countless magical cycling moments. The start was the usual opening short time trial. It was just over six miles and former world champion Rudi Altig was the winner, covering the distance in a fraction over 13 mins. Meckx took second place just 7 secs behind him but failed by that amount of time to take the first yellow jersey.

He had desperately wanted it to ride into his own territory

the next day when the first stage proper began from Roubaix to Woluwè St Pierre on the outskirts of Brussels. It was here that Merckx had spent most of his life, where he had grown up, living above his father's grocery shop in the suburbs of the Belgian capital.

If he did not have the jersey then the next best thing was to win the stage, but the whole field, 130 riders, were massed together over the last two miles and though he fought hard for victory it went to the Italian, Marino Basso. It was such a close thing at the line that only a photograph could really split the charging group and there, in it, was Merckx in fifth position and giving his all, just a length away but behind Basso, Dutchman Jan Janssen, Belgian champion Roger de Vlaeminck, and another Belgian, Peter Nassen, in fourth place.

Later that same day came the team time trial in which his Faema squad worked like trojans to take the all-important victory which gave Merckx the yellow jersey. If he had wanted it earlier he was happy now to wear it in front of his friends and neighbours as the race left the next day.

Merckx was to lose it immediately to his faithful team mate, Julian Stevens of Belgium, who won the stage into Maastricht. Stevens wore the jersey for the following two days after he had chased the still formidable Rik Van Looy into Nancy on the 5th stage from Charleville. Van Looy, even at 35 years of age, was capable of pulling off a victory and he did this in the grandest possible manner, breaking away alone with over 60 miles to go and finishing just 42 secs ahead of Stevens, the rest of the field coming in shortly afterwards.

From Nancy to Mulhouse, where Agostinho of Portugal won the stage, the leadership changed hands, Frenchman Desire Letort taking the jersey after finishing with the leading group which also contained Eddy Merckx but the first real day in the mountains was to follow.

The stage finished at the summit of the famous Ballon d'Alsace and it was on the lower slopes that Merckx made the first of the attacks which lasted throughout the Tour and eventually gave him victory. On that giant climb Merckx was

Simpson (*left*) wins the 1965 London–Holyhead from Elliott (*right*) and Hitchen (*centre*). Note Elliott's fingers on the brakes! *See* Chapter Eleven

The decisive move. *Left to right:* Lewis, Metcalfe, Sandy and Moore. Away for over a hundred miles on Stage 7 of the 1969 Tour of the West. Lewis won this Plymouth–Weston stage with Metcalfe taking overall victory. *See* Chapter Fourteen

Atkins triumphant on his home ground at Coventry, taking his first professional Cyclo-Cross title. *See* Chapter Fifteen

Two dominant 'Cross men. Mernickle leads Atkins (*centre*) in atrocious conditions in the Bagshot Scramble as they lap one (*left*) of many others in the event. *See* Chapter Fifteen

away with a group which gradually grew smaller as the steepness became more apparent.

About two miles from the top Merckx accelerated, giving Altig who had grimly been holding his wheel, no chance at all. Galera of Spain took up the running but he, too, made no impression and finished second, nearly a minute down on the young Belgian. Altig hung on to take third place almost 2 mins in arrears, Roger De Vlaeminck came in next over 4 mins down, a handful of seconds ahead of a group which contained most of the fancied men.

Merckx took the coveted yellow jersey at the end of that stage and never lost it again. He guarded his lead successfully the next day and then, at Divonne-les-Bains, won the five and a half mile time trial round the lake, turning the tables on Altig who was second, just 2 secs slower in 10 mins 40 secs.

Merckx had also retaken the lead in the points classification as they moved into the Alps for the ninth day – Thonon les Bains to Chamonix. French hearts were gladdened by Roger Pingeon, winner of the Tour in 1967, who beat Merckx in a close sprint to the line, having left the other favoured ones over a minute and a half behind. Merckx was second again on stage 10 which contained the climbs of the Col du Telegraph and the Galibier where the young Belgian took the prime. On the long run down towards Briançon, the wily Herman Van Springel, another notable Belgian who was second overall in the Tour in 1968, broke away to win the stage with Merckx heading in a group of 'names' just over 2 mins later.

He was now leading the King of the Mountains section and the second place, achieved ahead of Rini Wagtmans, Gimondi, Poulidor and Pingeon, consolidated his lead in the Points Classification. Never had there been such a race leader and his team comfortably ahead in the team race, too.

More mountains on the run from Briançon to Digne made no difference with Merckx now beginning to really run into amazing form. He won again that day, the eleventh stage, beating Gimondi in the sprint with the rest way down the road and well beaten yet again. Gimondi took his revenge on stage 12

G   97 winning it from Gandarias of Spain with that man Merckx in third place.

He could not be dropped and his hold on the jersey increased almost daily and at Revel, in the 12 mile time trial stage, he destroyed everyone again, winning easily in 24 mins 8 secs. Roger Pingeon was second but nearly a minute behind him.

From Revel to Luchon he popped up again in fourth place but this time over 2 mins down on winner Letort and second place Jan Janssen. So, everyone thought, he is human after all and the pace is telling a little but the very next day in the Pyrenees he swept them all aside in the most dominant manner possible.

The 17th stage from Luchon to Mourenx took in the climbs of the Peyresourde (5,127 feet), Aspin (4,984 feet), Tourmalet (6,937 feet) and Aubisque (5,602 feet). Merckx soared over the massive Tourmalet well in command and continued to increase his lead, descending the Aubisque to finish, in spite of a puncture, almost 8 mins in advance of anyone else. This was the final, crushing blow to any hopes nurtured by his closest rivals.

Even on the last climb of the race on the 20th stage where the summit of the Puy-de-Dome was the goal, Merckx still demonstrated his tremendous powers of strength and ability. Pierre Matignon of France, the 'lantern rouge' won the stage alone after holding a good lead with 40 miles to go. Behind him the big guns massed for the second place, Janssen, Pingeon, Poulidor, Van Impe, Gandarias, they were all there and so, too, was Merckx.

He trampled on them all as they took the steep climb even dropping little Paul Gutty, so far down on general classification that it didn't matter. It was another second place and another incident showing the complete dominance and ruthlessness of this great athlete.

Great Britain had their moment of triumph two days before when Barry Hoban sprinted to two successive stage wins but everything was dwarfed by this magnificent performance of Merckx. He went on to take the final stage, a near 23 mile time trial from Creteil to Paris, where the race ended at the Stade Municipal at Vincennes.

Trouncing the opposition yet again he recorded 47 mins 38 secs for the ride, putting France's greatest loser and still their most popular rider, Raymond Poulidor into second spot by nearly a minute. The race was over and all Belgium was jubilant for this was the first time one of their countrymen had won the Tour de France since Sylvere Maes took the honours in 1939, thirty years before.

What a victory this was! No one had ever won the Tour de France in such a manner, taking the King of the Mountains, Points classification, the 'Combine' (a new award involving all three jerseys, points, mountains and overall) and six stages into the bargain.

His rivals were strung out in a sad line, Pingeon nearly 18 mins down in second place, Poulidor third over 22 mins in arrears and so on. Janssen, who had won the Tour the year before, was 10th, nearly an hour behind. It was Janssen who had complained bitterly when Merckx was freed of the doping charges in the Giro but the final result was there on the finishing sheet and in the laboratories where the daily samples from Merckx had been sent for analysis. They produced a result exactly opposed to the manner he adopted to win – negative.

CHAPTER SEVENTEEN

TOUR SCANDAL

From my seat in a car just behind the leading group I saw a Spanish rider attending to the immediate needs of nature by urinating as he free-wheeled at the back of the breakaway as they rode towards Newcastle on stage 12 of the 1965 Milk Race.

There was just 30 miles to go and the break had just turned on to the A1 at Rushyford when the Spaniard relieved himself. It was not his action that worried me but a thought that had entered my mind. There was a popular misconception about hiding the traces of 'dope' by doing this so that when asked to give a sample at the finish nothing would be evident in it, the traces having been previously removed.

This was completely untrue of course, for traces of amphetamine-based drugs could still be found in urine samples up to 48 hours after taking an artificial stimulant. Nevertheless, testing for evidence of this nature was still very much in its infancy and, for the first time ever, random samples were being taken on the Milk Race and everyone knew what was going on.

This incident, coupled with the testing and another occurrence earlier in the day, had combined to make me feel rather worried about the situation. The earlier matter, taken on its own, had little bearing on things but, in joining it with the other items there seemed to be a somewhat alarming set of circumstances.

The first and then seemingly unrelated incident occurred when Santamarina of Spain broke away alone as the field began the notorious climb of Rosedale Abbey, sometimes called 'Rosedale Chimney' just 25 miles after the Scarborough start.

News of his progress was coming over the Tour Radio when

100

a sudden announcement that he had crashed into a car surprised everyone. What had happened was that the Spaniard had ridden straight into the back of one of the official cars parked almost off the road and waiting to carry out a time check.

The report came back that he picked himself up laughing, remounted and continued the climb. I remember looking at my colleague and co-announcer David Duffield and we just raised our eyebrows and remarked that it was 'rather strange'.

As Santamarina forged steadily ahead to take the overall lead on the road from the Polish rider Janusz Janiak whose 32 secs advantage had quickly disappeared, I must admit to not dismissing the sudden and almost inexplicable crash from my mind.

Perhaps I was looking for something else to provide some further proof for my own thoughts and when this very fine Spanish rider proceeded to water the A1 right in front of my eyes later in the day it seemed that my conclusions were being proved.

Proved though only to me and I could say nothing and do nothing. It was with a certain amount of dread that I awaited the results of the tests that had been going on and were still continuing for I felt that a scandal of this nature would be terrible for cycling, to say nothing of the effect it might have on the sponsors, the Milk Marketing Board.

They were my feelings then, feelings which, on considering all sides of the situation, soon changed.

Santamarina went on to win the stage and take the jersey, Janiak dropping to second place with Les West, riding for the Midlands, in third overall spot, having been with the Santamarina break on that 109 mile stage to Newcastle.

Only two days left now with more mountains on the penultimate and well-known run across from Newcastle to Morecambe and the final day from Morecambe to Blackpool via the Trough of Bowland. The Spaniard had already proved himself as a fine climber and there seemed little possibility of anyone wresting the jersey from him so late in the race. Lose it

101

he did through a dramatic and last ditch development which blew everything sky high when he and two other members of the Spanish team were disqualified for taking artificial stimulants along with Kenny Hill from Liverpool, the four of them receiving the awful news just before the start at Morecambe.

Standing there in the sunshine on the Central Pier at Morecambe amid the usual colourful scene about 45 mins before the start the whole thing seemed like a nightmare – it was almost unbelievable.

The Race Organiser, Harry Merrall, and the Race Director, Maurice Cumberworth, quietly called over the members of the Press and gave us an official statement on the matter. Immediately afterwards I ran to the nearest telephone, a kiosk on the pier to call the Press Association for whom I was covering the event. Imagine my frustration at being confronted with a phone which required four pennies in it before I could reach the operator for my transfer charge call to London!

Of course I didn't have any pennies at all but managed, with time running out, to borrow them from a spectator nearby, and phoned through the fateful news to London. My colleagues in the Press entourage had done likewise and the evening national and provincial papers were quickly at work with the sensational story.

All this time David Duffield had been left with the microphone in his hand, forbidden to release the information that eventually startled the cycling world! He coped bravely with the situation, even to the moment when Janusz Janiak of Poland was called up to take the leader's jersey from the Mayor just before the race moved off on its final stage.

Even then it was not all over in terms of excitement for Les West came through on that last leg to snatch a wonderful overall victory after starting the day nearly 2 mins behind the Pole.

By the time we reached Blackpool the news was out and the massive crowd along the Middle Walk gave West a tremendous ovation as he came in alone to take the stage and the overall victor's laurel wreath, finishing almost 3 mins ahead of the next rider home and Janiak, after West had collected the time bonuses on the climbs and the stage, over 5 mins down.

West had been tested four times during the race when over a hundred samples had been sent off for analysis, most of them being taken from British riders and only the luckless Kenny Hill, apart from the three Spaniards, being found 'positive' by the Chelsea College of Science and Technology, who carried out the tests under the supervision of Prof. Arnold Beckett.

Along with Santamarina who was found positive on two stages, Scarborough-Newcastle and Aberystwyth-Llandudno, were his team mates Angelo Usamentiaga, also twice found positive, and Salvador Canet. While only these three members of the Spanish team were disqualified, they all withdrew from the race.

Despite this overwhelming evidence the Spaniards maintained their innocence throughout as did Hill who could give no explanation of the traces of amphetamines in his sample either. Hill thought he might have taken it accidentally through using someone else's feeding bottle which could have contained an artificial stimulant unknown to him.

Whatever the case, innocent or otherwise, the facts were there and could not be disproved and all four suffered the indignity of disqualification, a move requiring courage and resourcefulness from the men at the top.

Harry Merrall and Maurice Cumberworth were brave men on Saturday 12th June, 1965, when the job they had to do was made quite clear. Cycling history was made that day and the sport became cleaner and better as a result.

Dope is a nasty word and a terrible stigma to a sport but at least cycling, through the efforts and courage of Merrall, Cumberworth and Beckett, coupled with the British Cycling Federation, began to put its house in order and, unlike some other sports, brought the problems into the limelight by their forthright action.

Cycling is probably the toughest of all endurance sports and thus lends itself naturally to the use of artificial stimulants. For many who took them they were a means of survival not an aid to victory but what a sorry state the mind as well as the body of such an individual must be in to do such a thing.

It is unfair and harmful and everyone connected with the sport can be thankful to the men who made their decision that day at Morecambe. One cannot forget either the part the sponsors of the Tour, the Milk Marketing Board, made in this black day for cycling sport.

Unlike many other organisations who might well have thrown up their hands in horror at such a happening, they stood by the decision makers and continued their sponsorship in the succeeding years.

Ken Hill served his period of suspension and came back to racing again, but the Spaniards did not return to the Tour in 1966 or in the immediate years afterwards. They swallowed a bitter pill indeed.

CHAPTER EIGHTEEN

SIX OF THE BEST

No British book about cycling in the Sixties would be complete
without mention of the return of Six Day cycle racing to this
country and the Skol Six Day staged at Earls Court in conjunction with the International Cycle and Motor Cycle Show,
was the forerunner of, I hope, many more.

The master mind behind it all was Dutchman, Charles Ruys.
To that man nothing was impossible and in the few years he
lived in Britain he turned cycling upside down and I, for one,
am happy he did. Always interesting, very out-spoken, highly
voluble, Charles Ruys was a breath of fresh air to British
cycle racing.

His voice sounded as though he gargled with scouring powder
and his knowledge of English was so good that he could bring
a blush to any Briton's cheeks! Ruys was not prepared to
accept that something could not be done, to him insurmount-
able problems were an immediate challenge.

I know that the sponsors, Allied Breweries, and sterling
work by Mr Hubert Starley, the Managing Director of
Champion Sparking Plugs, played a large part in the formation,
planning and financial success of the Six Day but it was that
Dutchman who really made it all possible.

I defy anyone to know what is going on when seeing a Six
Day bike race for the first time! It's worse, I've been told, to
actually ride one for the first time! When you eventually get
to bed all you can see is wheels and more wheels, above, below,
in front, coming fast, drumming on the wooden track all the
time. No sooner are you into one bend and out, the next is
coming up. The stomach flies away to the right and the arms
ache as they cling to the bars to hold the machine on the 40
degree bankings. No sooner is the stomach back than it goes

again when you reach the banking once more.

It is all speed, noise and colour. For the spectator it is quite magnificent and there is nothing in the world like a Six Day bike race. The atmosphere catches you, impresses you, excites you and it is this coupled with the stars of the board tracks that make it the finest sporting spectacle that money can buy.

Comedy, crashes, thrills, it's all there and so it was at Earls Court, the 3,000 spectators getting full enjoyment every night. Some of the world's greatest exponents of the small tracks were competing including the 'King of the Sixes' Peter Post of Holland.

By the end of 1969 Post had won a total of 56 Six Day events, in itself a world record but in 1967 he could not win the London Six for that went to the Danes, Palle Lykke and Freddy Eugen. Even so it is Post who draws the most attention both as a rider and a clown. Not, perhaps, so funny as Tom Simpson used to be or quite as crazy as West German Rudi Altig, he is still value for money.

In Ghent he always plays the part of the villain. He loves to stir the crowd and make them angry. Many is the time I have seen him lose a sprint and then, when his victor rides alongside to shake him by the hand, Post knocks the outstretched arm away with a great show of anger and disappointment. Immediately the crowd are on their feet booing and gesticulating, probably not realising that Post may have lost the sprint on purpose just to be able to enact his little scene for them!

Post only has to wag his finger and the crowd hate him. The Dutchman loves every moment of it and goads them into a frenzy, feigning fury or annoyance at the conduct of other riders or even the crowd themselves sometimes.

The big Dutchman is at his best before a hostile crowd. If they are not against him at first then he makes them dislike him! I have seen Post booed off the track and later cheered to the echo by the same audience for a superb piece of riding behind the motors.

Altig is a clown of a different calibre. He pokes fun mainly at the other riders, whipping off their crash helmets and throwing them up into the stands. I have even seen him throw a bucket of water over Post, completely soaking the Dutchman's cabin and the German's pranks and tomfoolery have lost him a few contracts before now!

The water incident was at Ghent in 1966 and Altig didn't stop there for he emptied a further bucket over Post's partner Fritz Pfenninger of Switzerland, while he was on the track! The Ghent promoter, Oscar Daemers, was quite furious and the proceedings had to be held up for some time to allow the track to dry. It was three years before Altig got a ride in the Ghent Six Day again!

Wednesday afternoons in Ghent during the Six are always a delight for this is the 'cheap' day of admission for school children and the old people. Racing is fast and exciting and also amusing with a large number of special primes to be won. These are usually in the form of bags of sweets, oranges, racing caps and the like, the winners traditionally throwing their prizes out to the crowd.

Post, always the villain, would sometimes take his prime, perhaps a 56 lb box of sweets, straight to his cabin, the act producing the most awful clamour of fury from young and old alike. It was then left for someone else to 'steal' the box when Post's back was turned and, amid great laughter, issue the contents to the assembled company.

Altig, of course, took a hand in all these goings on but it was the crates of oranges that the popular West German would try to win. Not only would he throw the major proportion to the audience but the remainder were utilised for other purposes. They were usually hurled across the track at other riders, bursting like hand grenades on the wooden surface with Post being the main target.

Altig's particular delight is to use them as one would use the ammunition at a coconut shy, the target this time being the rows and rows of beer bottles lining the bars in the track centre. Goodness knows how many he would break but he had an arrangement with the caterers and would happily fork out the cash for the damage. Needless to say it was a performance enjoyed by all and a feat of bike handling that had to be seen. It is not easy, even travelling slowly, to throw seventy or eighty yards, both hands off the bars, one used for the throw the other holding the rest of the ammunition, and to keep a good aim at the same time.

Along with a number of other riders Altig also likes to 'borrow' a hat or a handbag from someone along the front rows. On occasions it is a hot-dog or ice cream seller who is taken unawares and the contents of his tray are deposited on the track and quickly disappear!

The money for these items are usually forthcoming though woe betide members of the audience who shout their dislike of the riding! I recall seeing one such gentleman who had been voicing his opinions in loud terms, get his hat removed from his head with great speed.

His shouting turned to thanks as another rider brought him a beer and then his hat was returned. It had been filled with talcum powder unknown to the owner until he put it back on his head!

These moments of comedy are a necessity for the riders, for the constant grind of a Six Day, especially if one is not on form, can be miserable and boring. It is good for the crowd, too, and they have come to expect interludes of this nature.

The London Six Day, still sponsored by Skol Lager, moved to Wembley in 1968 where Charles Ruys again staged another excellent event. Post took it that time with his partner, Patrick Sercu of Belgium and these two fine riders won it again in 1969, but Ruys had gone and Australian Ron Webb was the man in charge.

Webb also made a good job of the race and Wembley is expected to house the Six Day for another three years with a special track to be built inside the arena. The old track, used at Earls Court, was not quite the right size and this has now gone to Calshot in Hampshire for the youngsters to use for training.

I think Six Day racing, or even Six Night racing, which was

the new formula adopted by Webb in 1969, is in Britain to stay, and it could be that we will not have long to wait before a British rider will score a victory at Wembley, the first since 1934 when Sid Cozens won with Piet Van Kempen of Holland. Tom Simpson was the last Briton to win a Six, taking the Brussels event in 1965 with Post, but I am thinking of a home victory.

Charles Ruys went back to Holland to promote events there and live in his own country. He also gave Les West and Graham Webb the opportunity of racing in Holland during the season back in 1966 and 1967. He made all the arrangements for them and there is little doubt that their period of racing in that country served them well.

British cycling owes a great debt of gratitude to that ebullient Dutchman who made the Six Day not just a possibility but a reality for Britain.

CHAPTER NINETEEN

'DOUBLE DUTCH'

The opening stage of the 1969 Milk Race was marred by a terrible and tragic accident which occurred near Liss after about 30 miles of the Worthing-Swindon stage.

Zdenek Kramolis of the Czech team, off the back through a puncture, was chasing to rejoin the bunch. He cut off a corner on a downhill run in his efforts to get back and crashed, at speed, into a lorry coming in the opposite direction. He was killed instantly, the first fatality the Tour of Britain had known.

The tragedy over-shadowed everything else that happened that day and the first stage win by Jasinski of Poland seemed a mere formality. It was not until the peleton moved out of Swindon en route for Northampton that the race seemed to wake up, everyone, for necessity's sake, putting the awful happenings of the previous day at the back of their minds.

At Abingdon, after 41 miles, a small break got clear. Engineered by the usually aggressive Doug Dailey of the Great Britain team, they soon held a two minute lead and were never caught again. Two Dutchmen were with it, Fedor Den Hertog and Popke Oosterhof, names that meant very little then but within the next fortnight, they became cycling household words.

Oosterhof won the stage, Den Hertog just behind him with Dailey being put out of a top placing by Panikov of Russia, both men having been dropped by the Dutchmen on the run in. Oosterhof took the jersey and the field of British, Irish, Dutch, West Germans, Poles, Russians, Finns and Swiss prepared for the team time trial to Oxford the next day.

Russia won the 42 miles undulating ride, clocking a fine 1 hr 39 mins 28 secs. Great Britain, with another good performance, took second place less than 2 mins behind them, relegating the Poles to third spot.

In the afternoon the race continued with the second half of the day's proceedings, a road race of 73 miles from Oxford to Malvern where it finished on the top of the notorious Wyche Cutting.

Enormous crowds were out all along the route and at Broadway, in the Cotswolds, the streets were so thickly lined that the people had spilled out into the road on both sides, narrowing it to just a car's width.

A small group was caught a few miles short of the long, uphill finish and it was every man for himself as the field began the climb up to the line. Dailey was there again and so, too, was the Dutchman Oosterhof. Josef Fuchs, a fine Swiss climber, joined them with several others, out of the saddle and going strongly.

About 250 yards to the line, on the sharp left hand hairpin, with a near one in six gradient, Oosterhof leapt away to take his second stage win with Fuchs second and Dailey third. Den Hertog was not far behind his compatriot who increased his hold on the jersey.

It was the mountains of Wales the next day, 111 miles from Malvern to Porthcawl, and while one expects a few ups and downs on the general classification on such a stage, the happenings that day could never have been predicted.

With the skies overcast the field set out and it was not long before the Russian, Nikolai Gontjurov, holding sixth overall place, broke away alone. He was quickly joined by Den Hertog and the ever-aggressive Pole, Josef Mikolajczyk, and an escape was complete.

Through pouring rain the trio increased their advantage along the narrow country roads and were over 2 mins clear as they turned on to the Ross-on-Wye by-pass with only 16 miles covered. A long stretch of dual-carriageway, almost 20 miles of it, then faced them and it seemed certain they would be caught by the bunch.

Once on the by-pass the main field began a series of attacks into the cold wind and rain, echeloned out from gutter to gutter. For a few miles the break was being held and there was every indication that it would come back despite blocking and sitting in by the three nations represented at the front.

Then, out of the blue, or rather the grey, race officials neutralised the bunch. A build-up of traffic at the back was beginning to embarrass them and, with the bunch spread right across the road there was no way for it to get past. How can one ever hope to run a cycle race under these sort of rules?

Traffic squeezed by, making it more dangerous in the wet conditions and showering the cold, muddy bunch with spray and grit. I have often thought it more dicey to have vehicles overtaking than to contend with approaching traffic, particularly when dealing with motorists who have never seen a cycle race before.

By the time the chaos was sorted out the bunch had slumped to a six minutes deficit at the end of the dual carriageway where some of the traffic, particularly heavy lorries, began to slow everything down on the narrow roads near Raglan.

Now it was the traffic in front that became an embarrassment but it meant little to the fast-moving trio ahead who were still working well together. Through Crickhowell after 50 miles and they were starting the first climb of the day, three and a half miles on Myndd Llangatwg.

They were at the summit as the bunch began to ascend the lower slopes such was their lead but the Russian crashed on the steep, dangerous descent and, though not badly hurt, lost contact and was eventually swallowed up by the bunch.

Den Hertog and Mikolajczyk plodded on, the weather improving as they took the 50 mph drop into Treherbert where the race winds through some of the Welsh mining villages before taking the final climb of the day, Cwm Parc. Chasing groups were now moving forward but still unable to create much impression on the leading pair.

On that last climb the Dutchman forged ahead, knowing that Porthcawl was only 25 miles away. By now Mikolajczyk

A sad-faced Spaniard. Santamarina displays his useless leader's yellow jersey in a hotel room after his disqualification from the 1965 Tour of Britain. *See* Chapter Seventeen

The 'Flying Dutchman' at speed. Peter Post in the Earls Court Six Day 1967. *See* Chapter Eighteen

Successful breakaway. Mikolajczyk of Poland (*left*) with Fedor Den Hertog on Stage 4 of the 1969 Milk Race. The Dutchman went on to take the stage and overall victory. *See* Chapter Nineteen

'The Emperor', Rik Van Looy, scoring one of his last great victories with a brilliant solo ride to win the 4th Stage of the 1969 Tour de France. *See* Chapter Twenty

had nothing left and could not answer the Dutchman's pressure. Irishman Peter Doyle had broken clear of the chasing group and was riding steadily up the climb but with little hope of catching either man.

In sunshine now Den Hertog sped on like a man possessed to finish just over three minutes up on the brave Mikolajczyk with a fine effort by Doyle gaining him third place but nearly 6 mins behind the Dutchman. The next group to arrive was over 8 mins down and had a frightening run through Porthcawl where there was little police assistance.

Doyle was almost knocked off his bike by a car, riding on the pavement to avoid it, when he was about to turn left on to the seafront, less than half a mile from the line. Bad for one man it must have been worse for the groups who had to weave in and out of slow-moving traffic entering and leaving the town.

Den Hertog took the yellow jersey which he kept to the end. The Russians lost the team lead to the Dutch and slumped to third place behind the Poles. There seemed no end to the ability of the triumphant orange jerseys of Holland for they went on to take the next stage to Aberystwyth with Oosterhof recording his third win and comfortably holding second overall place behind his compatriot.

When Den Hertog took his second stage win at Nottingham the Poles had already gained the team lead by just under half a minute from the Dutch while Russia fell further back after an unprecedented occurrence in Wales when two of their men retired. It was a complete mix-up and showed their lack of experience and a mounting sense of inferiority. It was on stage 7 from Caernarvon to New Brighton when Panikov punctured and Gontjurov dropped back to help him.

Gontjurov was their best-placed man and should not have gone back for his colleague who suddenly decided it was all too much for him and packed! Gontjurov, out on his own did likewise, bringing forth the Russian Manager's comments later, 'They were missing their Mothers!'

In the mountain time trial at Scarborough, Den Hertog

H   113 shared the stage victory with Peter Doyle and the Dutch had a further success at South Shields when, to their great delight, one of the workers of the team, Jo Vrancken, won the stage.

It was Oosterhof again at Harrogate on the penultimate stage and this finally brought home the Dutch domination of this race. Den Hertog took overall victory and the King of the Mountains while Oosterhof was second overall and won the Points Classification. The Dutch won eight stages and missed the team victory by 5 mins from Poland.

One may well ask what had happened to the British while all this action was going on. They were around all right and, with a bit more luck, might have done better. Stage wins at New Brighton with Sid Barras and Caernarvon with the late Peter Buckley along with their fine second place in the team time trial all helped towards Great Britain's third place on the team general classification, just 10 mins behind the Poles.

Had Barras not been penalised ten minutes for dangerous riding in the group finish at Stoke, I think they would have done much better but the penalty knocked the stuffing out of them just when they were fighting back and closing the gap in the team event.

The winner at Stoke was Brian Jolly, riding for the second string England team. Jolly took the first of his three stage wins there and collected the 'most outstanding performance' award by a British rider.

One of the tragedies of the year was the death of Peter Buckley in a training crash the following month. 'Buckles' had finished the Tour in third overall place, some 13 mins behind Den Hertog and later went on to record a fine win in the Isle of Man amateur international event.

A Manxman, he gave his country their first gold medal in the Commonwealth Games in Jamaica in 1966 when he won the road race. The Island's sad loss was shared by all British cycling for he was a brilliant rider who had had a great future ahead of him.

CHAPTER TWENTY

'THE EMPEROR'

Rik Van Looy was born at Grobbendonk in Belgium on 20th December, 1933 and he was not quite 15 years old when he won his first race as a schoolboy in 1948. Over the succeeding 21 years his name has hardly ever been out of the lists of winners and a glance at the record books really shows what a truly superb rider he has been.

I use the past tense because I am sure that even the 'Emperor' himself will have to abdicate soon, content no doubt, with having probably the most illustrious career of any rider since racing began. From the time he scored that first victory as a youngster Van Looy has been first over the finish line 490 times, an average of just over 24 wins a year spanning 20 years of racing!

Without any doubt his prowess as a roadman sprinter earned him the title of 'Emperor' although it was being said at the end of the Sixties that even he, 'Emperor Rik' would eventually be deposed by Eddy Merckx. Merckx may well smash Van Looy's achievements but he can never take away the famous Belgian's name. It will take everything that Merckx has to equal those three magnificent victories by Van Looy in the toughest Classic of them all, the Paris-Roubaix.

In all, during the period 1954–69, Van Looy won a total of 15 Classics. He was 23 years old when he won his first, the 1956 Paris-Brussels, and 35 years old when he took the Flêche Wallonne in 1968, his last classic win of the Sixties.

It has often been thought of him as a 'wheel-sucker', a rider who sits in and does little work in a break, saving himself for the sprint. True, he has won many times in a sprint from groups both large and small but he has also come home alone, just as he did in the first Classic win at Brussels. Belgium had already been taking note of the name and Van Looy was to become 'Rik II', before being named the 'Emperor'. 'Rik I' was the great Van Steenbergen who won the first of his two fine wins in Paris-Roubaix in the same year as Van Looy had his first cycling win in 1948.

Looking at the records of the two stars it is not difficult to decide who is really 'Rik I' although Van Steenbergen was a much better Six Day man and, until the Flying Dutchman, Peter Post set the record of Six Day wins towards the end of the Sixties Van Steenbergen held it with 40 victories. Van Looy rode the winter boards and had several successes with various partners but, essentially, he was a man of the road.

His nickname of 'The Emperor' was an apt one for he was good-looking as well as athletic and, as a good professional should, always reacted well to the enthusiasm of the fans. He was also a good captain, generous with money when it was necessary to pay for services rendered by members of his team.

I have written about the Classics in Chapter 21 where Van Looy is mentioned because of his extraordinary achievements, mainly in winning 15 during a period of 12 years. These victories alone are enough to remember him by but there is much more in the racing of this super-star.

Without wishing to detract from the wonderful performances of Eddy Merckx the racing scene was a tremendously hard one when Van Looy began his long career. The men who were still at the front of the bunches when young Rik began his racing life were, perhaps, harder and more experienced than the majority that Merckx has had to face.

In dealing with a professional career that started at the end of 1953 after Van Looy took the bronze medal in the amateur road championship one has to consider the type of man that was in command during this time. Bobet, Robic, Kubler, De Bruyne, Ockers, Darrigade, and Van Steenbergen himself. Meanwhile the scene was changing and there were other riders like Poulidor, Anquetil, Simpson, Janssen and, as the seasons follow, Gimondi, Godefroot and even Merckx come into the double decade of the Van Looy success story.

Van Looy had won 113 amateur events and it was no surprise to the Belgians when he won the 1956 Paris-Brussels by 46 secs from Bernard Gauthier who had escaped from the bunch by just 3 secs to take second spot. Van Steenbergen headed in the 'peleton' for third place and the writing was on the wall for the bunch from that day onwards.

'Emperor Rik' became a legend with his three wins in Paris-Roubaix alone but let us just drool over those classic victories: Paris-Brussels in 1956 and 1958, Milan-San Remo in 1958, Tour of Flanders in 1959 and 1962, Paris-Tours in 1959 and 1967, Tour of Lombardy in 1959, Paris-Roubaix in 1961, 1962 and 1965, Flêche Wallonne in 1968, Liege-Bastogne-Liege in 1961 and Ghent-Wevelgem in 1956, 1957 and 1962.

If one was to accept that they were the only events he rode then it was a most remarkable achievement but, when one realises that he was racing throughout the season and had many other wins, some even more important, then his exploits seem almost incredible.

Van Looy, in 15 full years as a professional, won 377 events, including two world road titles and could not have been more than inches away from a third which would have equalled the highest total of titles by Van Steenbergen. Incidentally, it was the same year that Van Looy won his first Classic that he lost the professional road title to Van Steenbergen, 1956. This was the second time that Van Looy was to take the silver medal in the 'worlds' but the way he ended up with it in 1963 will be talked about for many years.

It was in Belgium, on a fairly flat circuit around Renaix and there was no disguising the fact that Van Looy wanted to win. He had taken the titles in 1960 and again in 1961 and the Belgian National team were supposedly chosen to assist him in his endeavours.

It wasn't so much that he lost it as to how he lost it and there are many stories about what happened that day. The plain facts of the race cannot be refuted, seen by countless pairs of eyes and without listening to anyone's 'description' of what took place.

A group of about 28 riders were together over the final two miles and nothing was going to split them, the speed right into the thirties. Van Looy, somewhere among the middle, tried to work his way to the front, not, apparently, finding any assistance from his compatriots.

Inside the last 400 yards 'The Emperor' was flying and winding out his big gear, using all his skill to force his way through the pack. He hit the front just inside the two hundred metre mark as observers saw another Belgian jersey sitting immediately behind him. It was Benoni Beheyt and as Van Looy, with his usual superb sprinting, having given everything he had in that dash to reach the front, began to ease at the line, Beheyt came alongside but several yards separated them. It must have been an unbelievable moment for Van Looy to find someone coming up on him and he instinctively moved across the road to try and fend off the attacker. He was too late. Despite his attempts to forestall his fellow-Belgian, Beheyt was over the line just in front.

As Tom Simpson told me afterwards, Simpson having been away earlier and caught by the others, it was very much a case of 'should I push him' or 'should I pull him' for Beheyt. In the end he decided on neither but his victory was not a popular one. It certainly did not do very much for Beheyt himself who won very few events after that and gradually disappeared into obscurity.

Exactly the reverse happened to Van Looy who seemed to gather speed and stamina as the years went on. In 1964 he won 24 events and then, the following year, reversed the figures, taking 42 victories including the unbelieveable total of eight stage wins in the Tour of Spain where he ended the race in third overall place.

He was a good stage rider but, as many folk hasten to point

out, the mountains were always his stumbling block. Strange then when one looks down the lists of past Tours of Italy to find that the winner of the King of the Mountains title in 1960 was a certain Rik Van Looy. He finished eleventh overall that year after taking fourth place and the Points Classification in 1959 and won a total of 12 stages in the Italian Tour during the events of 1959, 1960, 1961, 1962, 1963 and 1967.

In Tours of Spain he won 18 stages in the four occasions he contested the event, taking the Points Classification in 1959. The Tour de France also carries his name in the record books with the Points victory and four stage wins in 1963, taking seven stages in all but succumbing to this gruelling event either through retirement or elimination four times in the six years he rode the race.

You name it, he's won it from Rome-Naples-Rome to Paris-Luxembourg and the minor stage races bear witness to his power. The Tour of Sardinia was one of his favourites, winning it three times and taking 18 stages in the nine years he competed in it which also included a second and a third overall place. During the period 1960–63 he won two stages each year in Paris-Nice, was twice winner of the Tour of Holland, a winner of the Tour of Belgium and twice Belgian national champion.

What more can one say about this man? While Merckx may be carving out his own place in cycling history in the 70's Van Looy has already smoothed over the edges of his amazing lifetime on the bike when, even at 35 years of age, he could still produce a formidable performance.

One of the last times I saw him with a breakaway was in Paris-Roubaix in 1967. He was 34 then and reckoned by everyone to be past his best but there, mixing it with Jan Janssen, Rudi Altig and half a dozen others, was 'The Emperor' and the group were still together as they turned on to the Roubaix track for the lap and half to decide the winner.

It was so close at the line, Janssen taking it by inches from

119

Van Looy with Altig third and the cheers for Rik were the loudest and longest that day. It was almost impossible to think that that same man, who let loose that sudden burst of speed, right there before my eyes, won his first race nearly 20 years earlier.

CHAPTER TWENTY-ONE

THE CLASSICS

The fame and fortune that comes with winning a 'Classic' on the Continent is difficult to describe to the ordinary British sports follower and even hard to comprehend among some cycling enthusiasts in the United Kingdom. Perhaps the best way to try and compare a classic victory in terms everyone at home can understand is to liken it to a century at Lords, a try in a Twickenham international and a goal in the Wembley Cup Final all rolled into one.

One classic victory is enough to set a rider apart from the rest, enough to give him a better living with appearance money from Criteriums and advertising boosting his salary and bonuses which, in themselves, will have increased accordingly.

Towards the end of the Sixties there were twelve Classics in existence although the UCI regulations allow for thirteen. All of them are one day races and take place in various countries. There are two in Italy, the Milan-San Remo and the Tour of Lombardy; Holland, Switzerland and West Germany each stage one, the Amstel Gold Race, and the Grand Prixs of Frankfurt and Zurich while the others are all run in France and Belgium. The French have three very famous events, Paris-Roubaix, Bourdeax-Paris and Paris-Tours while the Belgians run the Tour of Flanders, Ghent-Wevelgem, the Liege-Bastogne-Liege and the Flêche Wallonne (The Walloon Arrow).

Classics have varied and changed about in the past 25 years. Ghent-Wevelgem was only a semi-classic in the early Sixties while Paris-Brussels was still being run. This race was eventually terminated in 1966, the traffic problem being too much even for the co-operative police forces of the respective nations. The Frankfurt event began in 1962 while the youngest classic is the Dutch Amstel Gold Race, put into the calendar in 1966.

All the events vary in their distance and terrain and usually take place at about the same time each year. Only Bordeaux-Paris, the longest of all the Classics, has changed its date recently, moving to early September instead of being held at the beginning of June.

The Paris-Nice stage race has always been termed the 'Race to the Sun' for it leaves Paris for the South of France in early March but the title is sometimes used for the first Classic of the racing season, the Milan-San Remo, which follows on almost immediately after Paris-Nice ends.

Italy also have the last Classic of the racing year, the Tour of Lombardy, known as the 'Race of the Falling Leaves' because it takes place around about the beginning of October. September has, in addition to Bordeaux-Paris, the Paris-Tours event while the rest of the Classics are heaped into a hectic period covering the end of March, April and part of May.

This gets away with interference to the Tours of Spain, Italy and France and the world championships so that, with semi-classics, other famous events like the Dunkirk Four Day, Tour of Luxembourg, Paris-Luxembourg and many other big races, all fit in to make up a pretty exhaustive season for the professionals abroad.

The Classics are followed fanatically by the public on the Continent with enormous crowds along their routes and live television coverage over the last 12 miles. It was in 1960 that the first full coverage of a classic took place when ORTF followed the Paris-Roubaix, better known as the 'Hell of the North' over its last 25 miles.

Cycling history was made that day not only by the presence of the television cameras which sent out live pictures on Eurovision but mainly because the screen was filled for almost the whole of the near-hour long broadcast by a young, almost unknown, first year professional.

His name was Simpson and the Englishman destined to become of the great names in cycling, had broken away alone as the race entered its final phase. The last 25 miles of Paris-Roubaix are run over the roughest, toughest and most terrible roads that the north of France can produce. The cobbles are like cottage loaves in places and the roads themselves mere dirt tracks at times as the route crosses the beet fields of Flanders.

Simpson was away on one of his courageous, foolhardy but epic rides that sometimes came off but often failed. He lost out that day, being passed by eight men in all with only a mile to go and finishing on the Roubaix track in ninth place. What happened then just goes to show what a Classic means to the people abroad.

Although Simpson did not win he was given a bouquet and asked to do a lap of honour on the track. He made the headlines throughout Europe, Britain excluded of course, and had half the Continent in tears when he was caught so close to his moment of triumph.

That ninth place, naturally through his wonderful solo ride, gave Simpson nearly as much publicity as if he had won and it put him immediately into the top flight and, equally important, into the hearts and minds of the cycling public overseas.

It was to be another year before Tom Simpson pulled off his first Classic victory, the first by a Briton since 1896. The event was the Tour of Flanders and while Britain's greatest rider to date went on to record three other Classic victories, each perhaps better than this one, it was his sprint win over the Italian road champion, Nino Defilippis, that proved his ability to use his head as well as his legs.

Simpson dealt a shattering blow to Italian prestige that day for they were banking on victory, the first Classic win for Italy since 1953. Defilippis was one of the finest roadmen-sprinters at that time with a great fund of experience behind him. Winner of the Tour of Lombardy three years earlier and with several stage wins in past Tours des France, he was undoubtedly the favourite when he and Simpson, well clear of anyone else, approached the finishing circuit.

This was a smallish loop which took them through the

finish line three times before the final sprint and Simpson had attacked with about five miles left, taking only the Italian with him from a group of nine men.

Try as he did on several occasions, Simpson could not drop the strong Italian and, as they reached the last kilometre, pressmen and public alike were putting the name of Defilippis uppermost. Simpson began his sprint early with the Italian immediately taking his wheel and sitting comfortably behind, ready to make the final lunge when it appeared necessary.

With about two hundred yards to go Simpson seemed to 'die' a little but he was foxing and as Defilippis shot by him, the British rider attacked again, coming up on the Italian's right. Having passed Simpson on the right it was natural for Defilippis to look for his adversary over his left shoulder.

He must have had a big surprise to find Simpson nowhere in sight and as he paused momentarily, in that split second that it took for him to turn his head, Simpson went by like a rocket to take the 1961 Tour of Flanders by less than a wheel!

Defilippis was almost beside himself with rage and disappointment and he protested at length that he could not see the finish line properly. True, the banner had been blown down by the gusty wind, but he had passed over the line three times before on that finishing circuit and should have known where it was.

The officials had no hesitation in throwing out the protest and Simpson had won his first Classic, fair and square, too. In talking to me later about the ensuing publicity he admitted that he had never realised what it really meant to win a Classic until that moment.

It was to be over two years before the Durham born rider, who lived in Nottinghamshire but adopted by Yorkshire, was to win another Classic. Indeed, he hardly had any major triumphs at all during that period, such was his ill luck. Countless second and third places, even in the Classics, were the best he could achieve but, as always during his racing life, he never gave up trying.

It was 1963 when Simpson scored his fine victory in

the 356 mile 'Derby of the Road' the famous Bordeaux-Paris event where the riders pick up a pacing motor-cycle at the halfway mark. He shattered the opposition that day, winning by over 6 mins on the next rider. He had already taken second place in Ghent-Wevelgem and Paris-Brussels and third position in the Tour of Flanders that year and went on to finish second in Paris-Tours.

In the following year he beat Raymond Poulidor to win Milan-San Remo after the pair had got away on the famous Poggio climb, a few miles from the finish on the Via Roma. What a splendid victory this was but perhaps his finest of all the Classics was his wonderful lone ride to win the Tour of Lombardy in 1965.

Wearing the Rainbow jersey of a world champion, Simpson was away with Italian Gianni Motta, exactly the same situation pertaining the previous year. In 1964 Simpson tired and, suffering from lack of food, got hunger knock, and arrived way down, being passed by most of the field.

It was a very different story in his world title year. Motta was dropped quite decisively and 'Our Tom' went on to enter the Como Stadium alone, over three minutes clear. This rounded off a good year for, despite abandoning the Tour de France due to injury, he had been third in both the Flêche Wallonne and Bordeaux-Paris, riding the latter event just a week after winning the London-Holyhead. (See Chapter 11.)

When looking down the Classic lists of past winners only a few men really come into the lime-light once or twice and then disappear. The majority are the 'Vedettes' – the 'Great Ones', whose names appear among the first three on numerous occasions and this is why these events are Classics, because they are so difficult to win that it calls for class and that little bit extra which only the best men can offer.

It is every bike rider's ambition to win a Classic. That statement in itself gives a fair indication of the monumental task ahead of a rider among the field of often over 150 competitors that start out on these tremendous races. Nearly all of them cherish thoughts of victory but there can be only one winner.

Perhaps the finest record in Classics to date is held by the great Belgian, Rik Van Looy, whose exploits span a 15 year period during which he won 15 Classics, including Paris-Roubaix three times. Van Looy is the subject of another chapter (No. 20) and most of his great deeds are listed there.

That remarkable Italian, Fausto Coppi, has his name listed many times but his ability could not gain him a win in most Classics, although he won Paris-Roubaix in 1950. Most of his victories came, naturally enough, in the Italian events, with a possible record number of five wins in the Tour of Lombardy. It is difficult to believe that someone can beat this particularly in the way that Coppi won them.

He took victory four times in a row, from 1946 to 1949, winning again in 1954 after having taken third place twice in the interim period. He won Milan-San Remo three times but that has already been equalled by Eddy Merckx whose wins came in 1966–67 and 1969. No one, though, is likely to better the achievements of one Costa Girardengo of Italy whose name appears no less than six times as the winner during the period 1918 to 1928. Add to that two seconds and two thirds in the same eleven years means, in simple mathematics, that he missed being in the first three only once in all that time.

Merckx, of course, is fast becoming another Van Looy. He took Paris-Roubaix in 1968 and was second the following year, 1969, when in addition to taking the Milan-San Remo for the third time, he also won the Tour of Flanders and Liege-Bastogne-Liege. Having already gained the honours in Ghent-Wevelgem and the Flêche Wallonne in 1967. Merckx is well on the way to becoming an all time great, if he can keep it up. Age is well on his side since he was only 24 years old at the end of the Sixties.

So, the man the newspapers abroad dubbed 'Monsieur Milan-San Remo' after his third win, has every chance of knocking Van Looy's great performances into a cocked hat. Eight Classics in four years; more than half the victories that his fellow Belgian had and still eleven years in hand! We shall see.

Van Looy's three wins in Paris-Roubaix are, in themselves, a tremendous sign of greatness. Above all, this Classic is probably the hardest and toughest in the calendar and Merckx will have a difficult task ahead of him to achieve this one. Only one other man has taken this formidable race three times and he had a hat-trick way back in 1909–10 and 1911.

This was Frenchman Octave Lapize and, while a number of men, including another great Belgian, Rik Van Steenbergen, have won on the Roubaix track twice, it will take a veritable giant to equal such deeds in modern times.

Bearing in mind the keen interest in time trialing in Britain I hope to be forgiven for including in this chapter some mention of the one really classic time trial on the Continent, the Grand Prix des Nations. While it was first run in 1932 it has become much more popular in recent years, particularly since the Second World War.

It used to be over 100 miles but the route into Paris, changed several times, has more or less become established at the distance of 100 kilometres (62½ miles) since 1956. In 1965 an amateur event was run in conjunction with the big professional trial and has continued with Peter Hill then the British Best All-Rounder, taking a very fine second place in that first year.

Peter Head was second in 1967 with another fine performance while a Dutchman, now known all over Britain, Fedor Den Hertog, (see Chapter 19) won it in 1969. The distance is slightly shorter than the professional event, the amateurs usually covering 75 kilometres. (47 miles).

It has always been something of a surprise to me that more British riders do not compete in this event for most of our riders begin their careers in time trials. It would certainly be an indication of our prowess over the tougher terrain towards Paris instead of the flat roads to Southend or up the A1 on the 'Borough'.

Closed roads for the 'Nations' would also mean the lack of 'suck and blow' of passing traffic which is surely helpful to the British time trialist. Such a test against the watch would bring

out the truth about time trials at home and the Road Time
Trials Council should be encouraged to send their best men
over to ride this event.

Certainly, as I have said elsewhere in this book, it would
bring this side of the sport in Britain much more publicity,
providing, of course, that we can win. It matters not really if a
British rider is beaten for the experience and the mere fact of
participating should be enough to aid improvement and
stimulate competition.

I mentioned this event also to bring in one name in particular, Jacques Anquetil of France. Perhaps it would be
sufficient to say that Anquetil won the Tour de France five
times, in itself a feat not likely to be bettered, but his name
also appears in the Classics, albeit only on three occasions.

It is in the Grand Prix des Nations list of winners that one
can really see what a truly amazing rider Anquetil was. He
rode it for the first time in 1953 and won. He won again the
following year and the year after and the year after that . . .

For six years in succession this lean, blond, unsmiling
Norman dominated the greatest prize in time trialing and even
then he continued to win again even in 1966 fourteen years
after he had triumphed the first time. In all he won it nine
times in those fourteen years, beating the best in the world,
men like Ercol Baldini of Italy, Rudi Altig and Felici Gimondi
with his superb style and constant pressure against the clock.

I remember Simpson telling me that it was an experience in
itself to be caught and passed by Anquetil in a time trial
and, as Tom ruefully admitted, it had happened to him more
than once! Simpson said that without having to look round
he could tell what was going on behind him at least a mile
away. The roaring of the packed crowds at the roadside would
get louder and louder and suddenly Anquetil was alongside
him.

It was only for a moment, only long enough for Simpson
to get a quick glimpse of the great man in profile as he
pedalled smoothly by, the sweat pouring from him and flying
back in his wake almost giving you a shower. There was very

little movement except from the legs, the rest of his body remained quite still and he rarely cut off any corners. Although the roads were closed Anquetil would always try to stay on the crown of the road, keeping well clear of the sides and gutters. It was here that any loose chippings, gravel or grit would have been flung by passing vehicles, while the centre was normally clear of such hazards.

As Simpson pointed out to me when the great Frenchman won the Tour de France in 1962 he won it in the time trial stages. Simpson finished sixth overall, just over 17 mins down and almost exactly that amount of time was the total time difference between Anquetil and Simpson in those time trials.

It is also interesting to see that the other famous Frenchman of recent times, Raymond Poulidor, won the 'Nations' in 1963 but it is nothing short of incredible that this man should have had the enormous following and adoration by the French crowds for he only won two Classics.

'Pou-Pou' as he was affectionately known to millions of fans was undoubtedly France's greatest loser and it was unfortunate for him that Anquetil proved one of his main adversaries, particularly in the Tour de France of 1964. I said unfortunate but perhaps it should be the opposite way round for while Poulidor smiled and waved to all and sundry, Anquetil was the reverse, rarely smiling, never staying round much to sign autographs and had only his fabulous cycling qualities to endear him to the populace.

Poulidor was unlucky at times and one must give him credit in that 1964 French Tour when he was only 14 secs down on Anquetil when they began the last stage, a time trial. His great rival won it by 21 secs and, with the 20 secs time bonus, took overall victory by 55 secs, the smallest winning margin on record to date.

Bad luck again for Poulidor when Anquetil did not ride in 1965 for the large, pleasant-faced Limousan was reckoned favourite. But everyone forgot about a young Italian called Felici Gimondi who had finished second that year, just ahead

I

of Simpson, in the Flêche Wallonne. Gimondi won the Tour and Pou-Pou was second again.

This was the start of the rise to fame for Gimondi who went on in the following year to win the last Paris-Brussels and also took Paris-Roubaix with a tremendous solo ride. He rounded the year off in the most splendid manner, winning the Tour of Lombardy but, like Poulidor, he has had to take a number of second places since because of a fellow called Eddy Merckx.

CHAPTER TWENTY-TWO

'FIASCO'

Supporters of the British professionals had high hopes of a good performance by the team that was to represent Great Britain in the Tour de France in 1967. Obviously Simpson, Hoban and Michael Wright would be members but this was a big chance for the home-based riders to show what they were made of.

Similarly, it seemed a good opportunity to gain some publicity for the new class in Britain in their second season and, since I had been elected as PRO for the professionals, I tried hard to arrange something special in Britain before the Tour began. I was a little worried about holding this position in cycling for, although I was voted into the seat in my absence, I felt that there was always the possibility of my being accused of bias or prejudice.

It was a difficult situation even though only an honorary task but I figured on carrying it out for the one year. My plan to publicise the 'pros' was to get Simpson and the other Tour de France team members over to ride in Britain just before the big event. Their presence would, I felt sure, bring a number of TV, radio and press people along for interviews and so, with the permission of the Professional Association Committee, got on with the job.

If I had known then how it was all going to turn out I think I would have resigned on the spot. The events that were selected for the 'foreigners' to ride along with the other British cash men were the New Brighton Criterium, sponsored by Players No. 6 and the Vaux Grand Prix on the following day, Sunday, both races coming just before the Isle of Man Cycling Week.

Things went very well. Players' put up enough money to

help towards expenses and provide a good prize list, Vaux Breweries also produced some extra cash over and above their very generous prize list of some £800 and ITV came in with a fee to televise the Saturday afternoon Criterium from the New Brighton Seafront.

I had been in touch with Simpson and he had made the arrangements for the others to join him and fly over to London, getting another flight for Manchester. Naturally their fares had to be paid and also getting them to Durham for the Vaux and then on to the Isle of Man with hotels in between. Additionally I had to lay on a special aircraft to meet them at Manchester and bring them over to Liverpool. This was to save time and to ensure they arrived ready at New Brighton for the broadcast.

While the private aircraft was a bit costly I even toyed with the idea of having them brought direct from London Airport, this avoiding the transfer to Manchester and then piling into another plane for Liverpool. It was a lot of money and we didn't have to much to play around with.

Television interviews had been arranged at Durham after the Vaux race and before the riders flew to the Isle of Man which was more good news. It did not provide any cash for the 'kitty' but it would obviously put a little money into the pockets of those being interviewed and would give cycling a few more moments on the 'magic box'.

Strange how things can go wrong. My one big worry on the morning of Saturday 17th June, 1967, was the weather. I was hoping for a fine day so that a good crowd would be present not only for the event sponsors but for television, too.

It turned out to be an absolutely gorgeous June day and, as I drove into New Brighton that morning there was hardly a cloud in the sky. Some nasty black ones were to come up later but while they had an effect on everyone connected with the events of the weekend they made no change in the weather. Looking back on that fateful Saturday I think if it had rained it really would have been the last straw!

The very competent New Brighton Organiser, Alan Williams, had things well in hand on the sea front where the short circuit racing was to take place but, like me, he had no idea of the impending disasters which were to strike as we both chatted in the changing rooms.

The first intimation that things were not going well was the non-appearance of quite a number of the professional riders and when Simpson and his party had not arrived by the allotted time it was obvious that trouble was on its way.

ITV's 'World of Sport' programme was having to be juggled around because there was nothing to show and in the end, what few professionals we had there rode a short event specially for the cameras. Still no Simpson and no word as to his whereabouts. Cycling was not coming over very well either to the countless viewers in their homes or to the many thousands who had made the trip to New Brighton and were now lining the seafront.

Eventually the foreign entourage arrived, well over two hours late but, good professionals to the end and even without their own bikes, they changed quickly, borrowed machines and rode, along with a few of the British riders who remained and who had to be told they would get money for doing so after holding a short argument on the start line.

The event took place although 'event' is hardly the word to use. Simpson was interviewed and everyone packed up to drive madly across country to reach Durham in readiness for the Vaux Grand Prix the next day. Had Simpson got to New Brighton on time then the depleted ranks of British professionals might not have mattered so much but, as things turned out, they stuck out like a sore thumb.

Simpson, Hoban and Wright had been caught up in one of those nightmare happenings that occur so infrequently. When they reached London from Paris they were told they could not board the Manchester plane because there was not sufficient time between flights. Apparently there must be a time gap of 45 mins on a transfer flight and they should not have booked on the Manchester plane at all. All the arguments came to nothing and even though the aircraft was still on the ground at London they were not allowed on.

The near-boycott of the event by the British riders was as a result of several factors. Built up by one of those special cycling whispering campaigns, the whole thing flared up because of jealousy and money. I was to blame in a way because I should have foreseen the possibility of this and, with a little more foresight, could have avoided such a situation.

In the first place the prize money on the programme did not split the cash right down the line. One big first prize and several smaller ones did not give the home-based riders much chance against the trio that were also competing. I agree with this and should have checked on the division of the money but, quite honestly, it never entered my head.

Rumours abounded about the kind of appearance money Simpson was getting and, of course, the British professionals were not receiving anything. True, Simpson and the other two men were being given some cash but it was not exorbitant, the total available just did not run to that. I should have realised all this and made arrangements accordingly but, once again, it never crossed my mind.

I think I overlooked these two very important items because of concentrating on the publicity value. I was so concerned with ensuring the success of the weekend and I really believed that the British based riders would appreciate the whole thing and react in the best manner possible.

It never occurred to me that they would carry on in the way they did. I could not understand why someone did not bring up these points before although the prize list did not come to light until the programme was printed. Even then it could have been changed had enquiries been made and the situation brought out into the open.

The professionals were completely right in their objections but I feel their actions in trying to bring it into the open were very wrong and they did themselves a disservice. I think, too, that the whispering campaign had included the fact that I was making a small bomb out of it and that didn't help either!

The only thing I managed to make was a near-ulcer and, thankfully, if anyone ever wants to take matters further, the balance sheets can always be checked. I felt completely let down after the fiasco and it was a bitter pill to swallow to find that I had worked so hard to make the venture possible for the very people who turned against it.

Worse was to come. After the shouting had died away Simpson told me he could not ride the Vaux next day but had to return to France. We had quite an argument then which continued to Liverpool and Manchester Airports and over a hastily eaten meal. I was very upset and cross about it but no more disappointed than Tom himself.

He had been contracted to ride a track event near Paris and, ever since he had been asked to ride at home, had tried desperately to get out of it. Even at the Airports he was ringing through to France but it was useless and he had to go back. What was worrying him most of all was that he might be suspended for not riding there and miss the Tour de France as a result.

It was a great wrench for him to leave for France when he had set his heart on riding at home and to ride in the county of his birth, Durham. Sunday proved just as bad as Saturday had for me when I was left to break the news to the packed streets of Wolsingham at the start to say nothing of the Vaux officials, press and TV.

The thousands that came to see Simpson stayed and watched the race and were not disappointed in a way for they saw a truly tremendous event. It was won by Michael Wright with Metcalfe and Lewis close behind, in a sprint finish after the three of them had been away over the last lap.

The race gave most of those spectators an appetite for they came back in the succeeding years. It says much for Vaux Breweries that they continued to sponsor the event after such a calamity had taken place. Naturally the money they had offered towards the Simpson party competing was returned to them since the main member of the group had not appeared and Simpson asked me to apologise to them and said that he would

135

ride in the race next year without any expenses or appearance money.

He died just over three weeks later and I often wonder how things would have gone had he let his heart rule his head over that French contract. Assuming that he had done as he wanted, stayed and ridden the Vaux, he would have been suspended and, therefore, not permitted to ride the Tour de France that year. If that had been the case he might well have been alive for that Vaux event of 1968.

CHAPTER TWENTY-THREE

THE WORLD WAR CYCLING CHAMPIONSHIPS

Demonstrations, unfortunately, seem to have become a part of our lives but those produced by the Czech people in Brno during the 1969 world amateur championships were probably the most effective of any ever staged for political purposes.

The championships must have been a great embarrassment for the Czech Government and the Russians, too, coming as they did during the period of the anniversary of the Russian invasion the previous year. There was bound to be trouble and the influx of Western journalists for the events also created some problems for those wishing to keep matters private and confidential.

First indications of the disturbances to come was the reception for the Russian flag during the opening ceremony at the Brno Stadium. A storm of whistling and booing greeted this standard bearer and this method of showing disapproval was continued later in the day for the first event of the championships on the track, the kilometre time trial.

All other countries received the usual acclaim from this very sporting crowd but when Agapov, the USSR contender, came out to ride the noise began and even increased in its fury when he had the temerity to smile and wave to the packed stands at the end of his ride.

Every day the same treatment was meted out and the all-Russian final of the women's 3,000 metres pursuit proved a classic case with the audience completely ignoring the event, chatting away amiably to each other as though there was an interval in racing.

Pride comes before a fall is the old addage and it was very much so at the end of the match when Raisa Obodvskaya, a bricklayer's labourer, started her lap of honour. As the whistles grew louder she rode up the banking out of the back straight and thrust out her tongue at the crowd. Their fury turned to cheers of sheer delight when she slid suddenly down the steep slope to crash at the bottom, having forgotten to keep moving with the result that gravity took over the situation on behalf of the Czechs.

Frenchman Daniel Morelon qualified as a national hero on the night of the sprint final when he beat the giant Russian, Omar Phakadze in two straight matches. Phakadze withstood the storm of abuse and whistles very well and his philosophical approach to the hostile reception had to be applauded.

From various sections of the stadium coins were thrown at him, the only acts of actual violence, incidentally, during the whole championships. Through the USSR Federation President, he told me afterwards, 'I didn't keep the money. It was not worth very much!'

There were, as in every world title bid, many moments of genuine excitement and one of these was in the tandem quarter finals when the previously unthought of and certainly un-noticed Americans Tim Mountford and Jackie Simes put out the much-favoured Italians two to one.

They really rode well and the Italians must have had a terrible shock after winning the first run. On those last two runs, throwing the machine about in a most spectacular and hair-raising manner, Simes and Mountford, much to the delight of the Czechs who love cheering the underdogs, over-hauled the Italians on each occasion to hit the line just ahead of them to go through to the semis.

They came unstuck then, losing a place in the final to the West Germans Jurgen Barth and Rainer Muller. In the other semi-final match the Olympic champions, Frenchmen Morelon and Trentin were surprisingly beaten by East Germans Jurgen Geschke and Werner Otto who went on to take the gold from the Westerners.

In the ride for the bronze the Americans went out to Morelon and Trentin, who really made mincemeat of them and the French were a joy to watch in every section of the tandem event. Trentin, suffering from a cold which had kept him out of the kilometre, may have been the cause of their downfall but they still managed to delight everyone, even in defeat.

Perhaps the most amazing thing of all was the tandem the French used. They have pushed this same wreck of metal – that's what it looks like – around the tracks of Europe many times and I still cannot understand how this scarred and rusty looking frame has managed to hold together at the punishment it gets from those four powerful French legs at around 40 mph.

The tandem event was only introduced into the world championships in 1966 but there are no doubts as to its success. What a pity it is that there are so few tandem events in England. Promotors just don't seem to cater for them on the tracks in Britain and, as a result, there are no riders to try their luck at this fascinating, spectacular and dangerous section of the sport.

The team pursuit event proved another thriller with some very close matches but none compared with the final between Italy and the USSR. All through the series the sporting crowd gave their encouragement and appreciation to the teams with the exception of the red jerseys of the Russians.

The Stadium was packed for the final night and, right from the very first half lap of the team pursuit, it was obvious on whose side the roaring stands were – Italy. Those blue jerseys could not have had a better reception or vocal encouragement if they had been in Rome or Milan. The contrasting noise on the opposite sides of the track as the teams battled it out were fantastic. 'I-talia, I-talia,' screamed one side of the track as the Russians received the bird with thousands of piercing whistles, as they thundered down the other straight.

The clamour continued, growing louder as the distance got less. Italy took a first lap lead, held it to go nearly 2 secs up after three laps but then it came back. Slowly the gap closed and, with the bell ringing for the last lap the Russians took the lead for the first time by 0.18 and ran out winners by a fraction under 6/10ths of a second to the dismay of the Czechs.

The Stadium went down like a pricked balloon and a terrible silence descended on the place. Within 5 mins the stands were deserted as the bitterly disappointed crowd staged their last demonstration on the trackside, a complete boycott of the medal ceremony.

It can never have happened before. Just the press, officials and team members in the centre of the concrete bowl were present as the last national anthem for the track events was played. It was an eerie feeling and the teams, France having taken the bronze from the Czechs, did not come out to do a lap of honour. There was no point in it with no one there to honour them!

The rest day on Friday 22nd August was approaching and there was rumour and speculation as to what might happen because that was the actual anniversary day of the Russian invasion just a year before. During the events on the track a Doctor Somebody or Other introduced himself to me with a handshake, bow and a slight click of the heels. He explained that the organising committee were arranging a special garden party for senior journalists, champagne etc., at a place about 30 kilometres outside Brno, on the Friday, and would I like to attend?

It was fairly obvious that the idea was to get me and as many other press men out of the town that day in case there was trouble. I pointed out to him that I would have to contact my newspaper on the Friday to write a preview of the two road races which were to take place on the Saturday and Sunday.

He said he would let me know if he could arrange a telephone for me but never contacted me again and when the fateful day arrived I was free to observe the Czechs' reaction to the oppression. The only other British journalist there was Mike Hughes, the European Sports Editor of UPI, himself a cycling fan and we decided to team up for the day.

We also had a West German journalist, Karl-Heinz Sobel, with us for much of the time, all of us staying at the Hotel

Continental along with all the other press men covering the championships.

It was like a Sunday morning as we strolled across the Red Army Park and on towards the Liberation Square. The sun shone and hundreds of people were in the streets because most of the workers were holding a token strike that day which included boycotting the trams.

The first indication of trouble to come was that all entrances to the Square were quickly being sealed off. A water cannon and baton-wielding militia had already cleared the area and the Square was gradually being filled with half-tracks, armoured cars and troops. This seemed to be the headquarters of operations and things got worse as the day wore on.

Mike and I tried, by showing our passports, to get through the Square to the other side, asking police and militia on several entrances but the answer each time was to go round the long way. The crowd who had been removed from the area had not been doing anything they were just standing around and not even shouting when they were literally thrown out.

Within a few hours it was like a war. Tear gas, tanks, baton charges, when Mike and I learned to run really fast, and there were sporadic outbursts of firing. This was mainly directed over the heads of the crowd but several were hit and, from what we could gather in the confusion, four killed.

Our eyes red and watering from the tear gas as we tried to establish the facts from the packed pavements around us, a difficult task since only Czech was spoken with a mere smattering of German or French.

Incongruously, we wandered among the people, saying, 'Does anyone here speak English?' Amusing looking back on it but it wasn't very funny at the time. The Czechs just shook their heads but knew who we were and they kept shaking us by the hand and it was hard to tell if they were crying or if it was the effects of the tear gas.

The tanks came rumbling in next and, as darkness came down the situation worsened with barricades being erected with over-turned cars, planks and anything that came to hand while the cobbles in the streets were ripped up for ammunition.

Despite the situation Mike and I managed to get stories out. I telephoned mine from the other big hotel in Brno, the International, dictating it straight 'off the cuff' for fear of being caught with written proof in my hands.

I stayed at the International on the Sunday night as my paper wanted me to remain there and keep watch on the situation. I had to apply for an extension to my visa which expired on the Monday and I was told that morning I would have to apply personally in Prague but I was not permitted to stay in Brno any longer.

This was the final straw as my telephone had been tapped and my room searched while I was out on the Sunday evening, although nothing was untidied there was ample evidence of things being moved around. Perhaps just a case of having the 'frighteners' put on!

Mike and I left by car for Vienna that day but not before we had tried to witness one of the funerals of those shot on the previous Friday. It was to have been in secret but 'inside information' gave us the time and place. It never happened because I think they knew we were still hanging about and we left by car for the border, drinking a large beer as soon as we arrived in Austria!

The excitement of the championships faded for me after that but I still recall the American Audrey McElmury, producing a wonderful lone effort in the pouring rain to take the women's road race gold medal.

A great sprint by young Bernadette Swinnerton, gained Great Britain the silver from a charging mass of riders and there was a fine eighth place by Pete Smith of the Clifton Cycling Club, later to join Clive Stuart Cycles Professional team, in the men's event on the Sunday when the British riders were undoubtedly the chief animators of the race.

With Mike Hughes very busy during the track events I had not spent much time with him in the early part of the championships and had been mainly in company with the Dutch press and radio men.

One of them interviewed me on tape during the amateur road race, saying that I had been the life and soul of the party until that fateful Friday but had since been more serious and I can well remember replying, 'That was when the world whistling championships were on. When it turned into the world war cycling championships it wasn't funny any more.'

INDEX

Index

Index